I'm a Changeling see me change

I'm a Changeling See Me Change

(The Eddie Fisher Story)

By

Eddie Fisher

Dedication

I would like to dedicate this book to my angel. Who is my mother.

Acknowledgement

Most of all I would like to thank my friend Paul who I met in Thailand and who encouraged me to finish this book and also took many many hard working hours to put the book in order and publish it online which I may have never done. This story sat in the dust bin of my computer for many years. I would also like to acknowledge and thank my friend Karl who took the time to type out everything for me that I had dictated onto tapes.

Contents

Introduction

I was born in the fifties and Life Began idyllic. I was young and happy my parents were kind and loving. I was raised in a Christian school and have no regrets about that it was a good way to live.

But as I got older I began to rebel against everything and everyone who ever tried to tell me what to do and my path begins to change to one of danger, excitement, sometimes fun and sometimes very injurious to myself and to those around me.

As you read in this book, you will see details of what happened during this period of time. Completely destroyed my life and alienated everyone around me. I was moving from city-to-city, lover to lover, bar to bar, job to job.

About the author

I was blessed with good schooling and became a certified court reporter at the age of 21 and worked hard all my life. Also helping to develop real-time closed captioning equipment for the hearing impaired and working on the many high-profile jobs.

During this period of time my drinking took me to places that took away any promise of a good life or a marriage or children which I have never had to this day.

Thankfully, on April 10th 1997 a new chapter in my life begin a journey which changed my life 100% where I began to live with some Integrity, clean and sober and respectful. I was able to build a new life with the help of so many others for whom I will be grateful for as long as I live.

I was able to heal with my parents and sister.

My gratitude extends to friends all over the globe.

If reading this book helps one person it has been

worthwhile to publish it.

I hope the details revealed in this book are not too distasteful and that you enjoy the read of the good, the bad, the ugly and the miraculous.

Blessings and peace to all

CHAPTER 1

REBEL WITH A CAUSE "The Childhood years" Arson, Theft, Lies and Runaway.

Hello. This is Ed Fisher, born January 13, 1955. I am going to record the story of my life, starting from the beginning. I might jump around a little bit.

So when you tell a story about your life, I guess you start from the beginning. I was born in Pasadena, southern California, and my mom and my dad were really good parents, but from the very beginning I was a rebel.

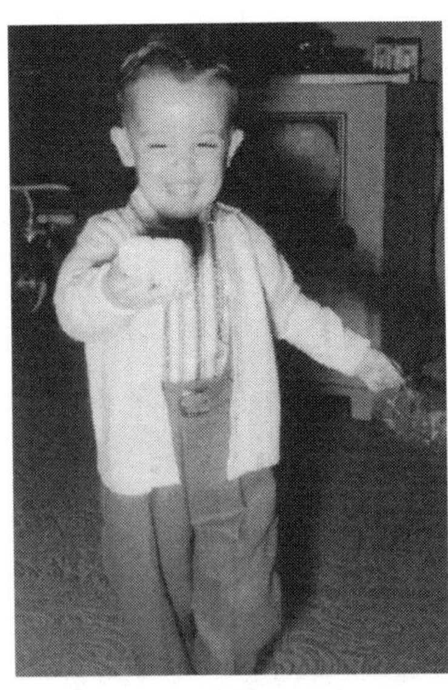

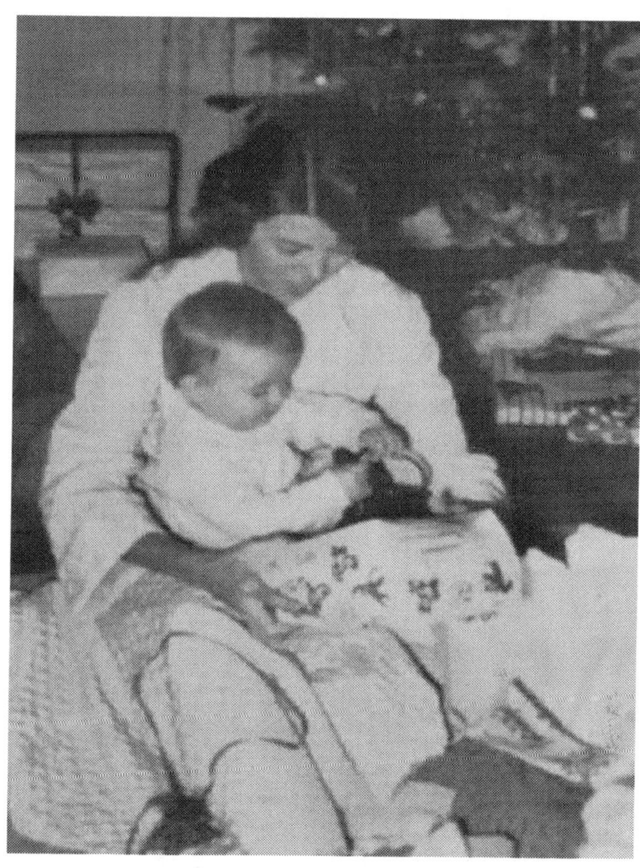

My Loving Mother and Little Eddie

So I guess I should maybe just start from when I started getting into trouble.
How did this cute little kid cause so much trouble?
But I was a good little kid and I was sent to a Lutheran school. I went to a Lutheran school every day for the first four or five years of my schooling and I went to a Lutheran Church and I enjoyed it. I did like to fight. I fought with a lot of kids, and I was real good at sports and I was pretty smart.
As with lots of children, you will hear the expression, he has so much potential. I used to get in a lot of trouble at school from the time I was little.

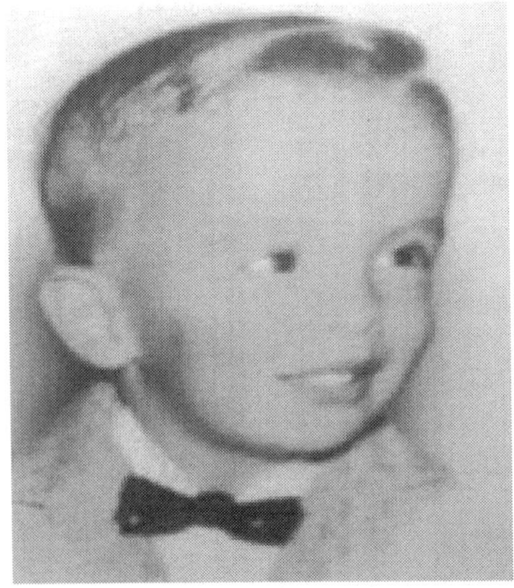

Me and my Sister

Even in kindergarten, first grade, second grade, third grade, the school I went to, they used to spank you with a wooden paddle, so that stands out to me pretty clearly.

Me and my Sister

By the time I was in fourth grade, well, even before fourth grade, I accidentally started an arson fire. There was one vacant lot in my neighborhood, and I just started a little fire to play around with a friend of mine, and the next thing I knew, it had grown way out of hand, so I ran. And then some fire trucks showed up while this fire had spread to two houses and was burning down their fences. Fortunately, the houses didn't get burned down and, of course, I got caught. And I was a seven-year-old kid, so they just pretty much reprimanded me.

It wasn't long after that I thought that the world was kind of picking on me, especially my dad, and I wrote a little note that my mom has saved to this day, and I can't remember exactly what it said, but something to the effect: I am leaving home because I don't like dad.

And I ran away and I went to a place across the street we used to call the frog pond. There was a sewer tunnel up there, and I went under that sewer tunnel. And after a few hours, I got hungry, so I left and I went to a little five-and-dime store. I think it was called Woolworth's. And I went to that five-and-dime store and I stole some candy and toys, or whatever I stole, and I got caught and the police showed up, and so that was my first of many rides in a police car at seven years old.

The police gave me a ride home to my parents and I was punished very severely. And I remember it quite clearly, because the window was open or the drapes were open, and as my dad was whacking the crap out of me, some of the neighborhood kids were out in front watching.

So here I am seven years old, already have had my first ride in a police car. I guess I will just jump a little bit. Like I said, I skipped a grade in that elementary school, so I was younger than everybody in my class. I started public school in the second half of the fourth grade, and immediately I began to get in fights with anybody that I thought threatened me, and it helped make me friends.

You know, people could see I wasn't afraid of anybody and, you know, I got in trouble and I fought kids that were older than me, and I was kind of popular.

I was a very good athlete. I also joined the YMCA and I played baseball, football, basketball, field and track, swimming, diving. I was very, very involved and enjoyed it a lot too.

I loved the competition. I probably loved it too much, and I spent every waking minute outside of school playing sports around my house.

I do remember an incident in elementary school where I decided I was going to become a little thief, and what I would do in the winter time, even though the winter time isn't that cold in southern California, I was in Sepulveda at the time and I went to Balboa Elementary School. And I would walk along and I would see a purse and I would throw my coat or drop my coat on it, and then as I picked up my coat, I would walk away with the purse that was underneath it, and I stole quite a few purses that way.

I became an accomplished little thief. And eventually, I got caught for that also. So I am just a trouble maker from day one. And, you know, my parents have a lot of rules and I always know when I break them I am going to get punished, and punishment means getting whacked with a paddle. And whatever the rule was, I broke them. I broke them all.

Anyway, I thought I had a pretty fun life. Like I say, we had this frog pond across the street. It was a big corn field, and then at one point, there was a stream and there were frogs and lizards and I would play up there. As I got a little bit older, I got a motorcycle, a dirt bike, and we used to ride bikes up there all the time, and when the police came chasing us, we were good at getting away from them. You know, I would ride that motorcycle up and down the frog pond and around the cul-de-sacs and the police never caught us. We thought it was a blast.

Chapter 2

SNAKES, LIZARD AND GUNS

I became infatuated with lizards and frogs and tadpoles and insects when I was young, and I spent my summers and weekends running around the hills of Chatsworth and also in the frog pond across the street from me off of Balboa Avenue chasing lizards and frogs. And I had cages at my house filled with lizards and snakes, and it was just a lot of fun. And even as I got older, when I became a teenager, I collected snakes.

I turned an entire area on the side of my house, I would say it was 20 feet long and six feet wide, I lined it with plastic and I put I don't know how many hundreds of lizards back there, lizards, scorpions, maybe I don't think tarantulas, but if I had some I would have put them back there.

I had a little pond back there too, a little, tiny pond area. Another friend of mine, the Martinez brothers, we kept a little pool at their house that we kept alligators in and snakes. And they were older than me, so they would drive. We would drive down to Palm Springs and go out on abandoned roads late at night.

I would sit on the hood of the car with a flashlight and we would find snakes that would come out on the road. They would gravitate to the heat of the road late at night, and we would catch snakes, all different kinds. I loved king snakes. I had a collection of king snakes. But I also started keeping rattlesnakes in my bedroom, and that kept my parents out.

I also used to feed the snakes, which was always exciting to feed mice to snakes, but also king snakes will eat other snakes, including rattlesnakes, so we had many rattlesnake-king snake wars, which was very interesting.

And I don't know. There was a time in my life, maybe when I was 13, 14, 15 years old where I thought that might be my future. I thought, I am going to be a reptile hunter. And I did a lot of business with pet stores. We sold lizards. Sometimes we would catch hundreds of iguanas and alligator lizards and stuff and we would trade and sell, and it was a lot of fun. It was a little bit of a business, but mostly it was fun.

Then later, I thought I was going to become a ranger and work up in the forest in Yosemite or the Redwoods. But anyway, back to lizards, snakes and playgrounds, I just spent hundreds and hundreds of hours on the weekends hiking in the mountains, catching lizards and snakes and really got good at it, and also out in the desert.

And as far as playing, in my neighborhood, we played. There were TV shows, but I was only allowed to watch TV maybe an hour a night with my parents. Sometimes I could watch some cartoons, but I had to be in bed most of my life before 9:00 o'clock at night until I was in junior high. I had a very strict upbringing, and we didn't have computers and video games.

Well, we did have pinball machines,

which I got to play at at the bowling alley sometimes, and I liked playing those. But I liked sports, you know, and I liked playing ball and softball and catch. And we had a game called Socko, which isn't soccer, it's Socko. And I am not even going to try to explain it, but we had a lot of different games, including even hopscotch and hide and go seek.

And we just had a lot of games, and the neighborhood played games together. We played a lot of games out in the streets, and there were always a couple of neighbors who had swimming pools, and we had swimming parties and barbecues. And so even though I talk about some of the strict upbringing and the church and the drinking and stuff, there was a lot of fun also.

I also got involved, my father got me involved in building model airplanes and flying gasoline-powered model airplanes and golfing. We used to play chess and cribbage with my father as a child. I became a very, very good bowler. I was involved in bowling leagues for many years from the time I was a small child until high school, and then I took up bowling again later in my twenties and got involved in amateur bowling sports and winning money on the weekends playing tournaments. So I really loved that.

When I was real young, I got into golfing and did a lot of bowling also. I became a very good bowler and a very good golfer, and I had a lot of fun doing that.

When I was about 13 or 14, my dad started going down to the Salton Sea on the weekends where my dad would sell real estate, and I would go down there with my dirt bike and ride my motorcycle and go to the golf course and go golfing. I had really a lot of fun.

And then after our relationship all went into the pot, you know, I became isolated from my family. I built a real nice Honda 305 and I used to ride that around a lot. I used to love riding over to the beach from San Fernando Valley over to Topanga Beach and back. I used to do that almost every day.

And I played golf until I was about 15, and I got in an argument with a high school teacher and he wouldn't let me on the golf team, so I quit and I didn't play again for 15 years, and then I took the sport up again in Boston and became a very avid golfer from about the age of

30 to 36, 37. I became very good at golfing.

And I quit again for almost 20 years, basically. I have maybe played ten rounds in 20 years, and I just started playing again in Thailand last year at the age of 57. Also, I just took up surfing at the age of 56, or trying to, at least.

And so back to my childhood, like I said, again, I had a lot of fun. I used to go fishing with my dad during the summertime, and the catching of the lizards and snakes and playing ball with all of the neighborhood kids. And so, yeah, yeah. It was a lot of fun, and riding bicycles.

At one point, me and Jeff Bassenberg and Ken, Jeff had an acetylene torch, and we sawed the forks off of the front of our bicycles when we were about 11 or 12 years old and we put extensions on them and turned them into choppers. So here we are, 11-12 year-old kids with our choppers, Stingray bicycles and sissy bars. It was very exciting for us. We thought we were a little chopper gang.

And then at a point in time playing with guns also. We used to go out to the Soledad Canyon, to the desert, and started playing with rifles and pistols .22s, mostly. And, you know,

13, 14, 15, finally at about 15, a couple of the guys had driver's licenses. We would go out there, and we had gotten involved and loving Clint Eastwood movies. And we were drinking beer and smoking cigarettes and shooting guns, and that's a dangerous combination.

And we even played a game, it was -- I don't know if it was cowboys and Indians or good guys and bad guys, but we would hide behind rocks and shoot at each other, and not to try to hit each other but to get close to the person, and I guess if you got within a certain distance of them, you know, he was dead or whatever.

And a couple of people got shot. One guy got shot through the leg. I think it was Ray Limbo or Paul Limbo, and Rick Perello got shot in the finger while he was sleeping by accident. You know, these drunken things happen. I believe Jeff might have even got hit in the leg.

But, you know, we did a lot of crazy things when we were young. And so aside you know, we weren't what we would consider good kids, but we had a lot of good fun. I really did have a lot of good fun growing up.

Just before my 16th birthday Me and a friend named Byron Raefelson were up in the hills by the frog pond smoking some weed. Might have been drinking a little wine too.

And we saw a motorcycle cop up there, and I was on my motorcycle, my Honda 305 scrambler. So I said, we better get out of here. And I had straight pipes on it, so it was a loud bike. And I was under the impression that this cop was chasing us, so I hit it and I hit it hard, and I lost him. And my friend, who was pretty smart, said: "Pull over. We have lost him."

But I didn't want to pull over. I kept going. And I got into a busy street and a plain clothes or off duty cop saw us and he heard about the chase on his cop radio, and they ran us down. And it was pretty ugly. My friend got in a fight with the cops, and we got brought into the Van Nuys Police division and arrested, and it was quite a scene. I forget when or if at some point, my mom picked me up, and I had to go to court and ended up having to go to some kind of meetings. It was kind of like alcoholics anonymous for juveniles. You get in a circle and you talk about your shit. That was kind of a scary incident.

My Triumph 650

And these same guys, you know, Brad Smart and Ken and Jeff, we all grew up together and then we were in the band together. We started going fishing a lot. We would go deep sea fishing and get drunk. And we started fishing on golf courses when we were golfing more in our I can't remember. I guess in our twenties.

Eddie on Triumph & Parents on motorbike 1947

We weren't golfing. We were just going to golf courses to fish. We found out that there were bass ponds on golf courses, and we would hike into them late at night up in Los Virgenes Canyon and West Lake. I mean, these were nice golf courses, and we would hike in late at night and catch bass.

I graduated from high school when I was 17. I had a lot of friends who went to Vietnam. Some of them died. Some of them didn't come home. My best friend's brother committed suicide. there was a lot of tragic things that happened, you know, as a direct result of drugs and alcohol.

Anyway, life was still pretty good for me at about 17. I graduated from high school and did the thing with college and the court reporting and eventually became a court reporter and became a drunk too.

CHAPTER 3

LOVE OF GIRLS AND LIQUOR

I got to like a girl. It was Barbara and Pam Wetzel. They were twins, and I think that Barbara was my girlfriend. I don't remember. I was so shy. I was scared to death to do anything. I would walk her home from school. That was about it. And that was in the sixth grade.

Anyway, I just remember that real clearly. I graduated from my elementary school, Dearborn Elementary School. It was a brand new elementary school and they built a brand new junior high next to it. In the seventh grade I started the seventh grade when I guess I was eleven years old. Eleven, twelve, thirteen. Well, I don't know. I was ten or eleven. I was pretty young.

But I did pretty well in that school and I started getting in trouble. I started hanging out with the kids that smoked cigarettes and I would smoke cigarettes occasionally, but I was still very involved in athletics and enjoyed that a lot. And eventually getting in trouble with my friends became a little more important than athletics, although I didn't say this. At this time, my father was away a lot. He was a flight test engineer and he was working at a place called Area 51 out in Nevada, but he couldn't tell us where he was because it was a secret project.

He worked on the U2 and the Blackbird, SR 71, I believe it is called. And he would come home on the weekends a couple of times a month, and he started teaching me how to golf and play chess and we did things like that. I took golf lessons and I became kind of a good golfer when I was a little kid.

My 19th birthday with Mom and Sister

And so that's what I did. I golfed and I rode my dirt bike and I caught lizards and snakes, smoked cigarettes and got in trouble. I had some other friends that were starting to use drugs and smoke pot and take pills, and I didn't want nothing to do with that, but I did find something else I liked when I was about thirteen, and that was called liquor.

And one day me and a kid name Brad Smart were at Terry and Gina Inser's house, and their parents were gone, and we broke out a bunch of bottles, probably three or four bottles of Scotch whiskey and vodka, and we had a chugging contest.

Now, I had had some beer or some champagne before at a wedding or something, but this was the first time I ever got drunk, and I lost my shyness and I was able to kiss Gina and do some things with her. And what happened was her parents came home while my pants were down to my ankles. I went running away fast as I could. About an hour or two later, my parents found me passed out near that corn field across the street from our house, and my friends were sitting with me. They didn't know what to do. I wasn't movable. My parents thought I was OD'd on drugs or something. They took me to the hospital and it turned out I had alcohol poisoning.

And I still loved it. I mean, I just you know, a funny thing with booze is, instead of saying, "I never want to do that again," I said, "I want to do that again, but I will do it different next time. Next time, I won't drink so fast. Next time, I won't drink hard liquor. Next time, I will just have beer or I will just have wine."

And I started drinking every weekend. That's what me and my friends did every Friday and Saturday night. We either got older brothers to buy us some booze or we would stand by a place called the Matador Bowling Alley, which was next to the gourmet liquor store on the corner of Balboa and Nordoff, and we would stand there and wait for a trucker or somebody who looked cool and asked him if he could buy us a couple of six packs of beer or a couple of bottles of Boone's Farm apple wine or strawberry wine. And then as I got older, it got easier to get booze.

Ed right about the time he started to enjoy booze. Things really changed.

Anyway, I am going to put in a little story here right now. By about the ninth grade, I was hanging out with this guy named Rick Perillo. Actually, I had been hanging out with Rick Perillo since the fourth grade, and we were real good friends. And he drank a lot and I drank every weekend with him.

And when we were about thirteen, we had a job of being I guess you would call it the art case monitor. We would walk around the junior high, at Holmes Junior High, and we would decide how art would be displayed and different notices would be displayed in different cases, display cases around the school.

And like I said, I was a regular cigarette smoker already at this time, so we would smoke cigarettes. And I used to carry these wooden matches with me that you could light with your thumb tip. And as we were walking back from the administration building after filling up one of the display cases, I was playing with this match and it lit and it started to burn me, so I threw it, and it ended up under a tree outside of a fence, and I couldn't reach it, because the fence was locked, and it started a fire. And this was not a small fire. I never got caught. The fire probably got to be 30 or 40 feet tall. Several fire engines showed up. It started to burn the administration building. It was real, real serious. That was something we didn't talk about, never told a soul about it. My mom doesn't know. None of my friends knew. Me and Rick Perillo were the only two people who knew about that. Rick died of alcoholism 45 years later at the age of 57.

I made it through the ninth grade, and

me and Rick, we didn't like some of our teachers, so when we graduated, we thought, how can we get back at the school? And so now we are in the tenth grade, and it is graduation day for the ninth graders a year later.

And we got on a dirt motorcycle with Rick had an axe and we ran across on our motorcycle, we ran through the graduation ceremony yelling and swinging this axe around, and some of the physical ed teachers and the principal and the vice principal surrounded us and tried to stop us, and we just rode straight through them and through the halls of the metal shop and out of the school, and we just thought it was hilarious. For us, that was fun.

And, in fact, thinking back even a little further, after I graduated from the sixth grade, me and my friend Jeff Basenberg, we took cherries bombs or M 80s from Mexico and threw them onto the playground of the school during their during or after their graduation ceremony. So it was just always getting in trouble for one thing or another.

But I did get out of junior high, only got suspended once. I got plenty of swats. They used to swat us in junior high too. Every time you got caught smoking or doing something wrong, you would go to the principal's office or to the physical ed office and you would get a certain number of swats, and they hurt. They hurt a lot.

So now I am in the tenth grade and we are drinking every Friday night before the football game. And we got a couple of friends that have a car, and now and then, the police were pulling us over, and they just would make us dump our beer out.

And we are not getting in a lot of trouble. We are having fun. We drank at the corn field across the street from my house. There is a little league field there too, and they have these dugouts and we would bring our beer over to the dugouts and we would drink before the football game on Friday.

On Saturday, we would find somebody's house whose parents were away for the weekend. We would play poker and pretend we are like Clint Eastwood, you know, smoking little cigars and playing penny, nickel poker and drinking our beer. And I don't know. At the time, it seemed like a lot of fun. And I wasn't getting in too much trouble, but I was getting in a lot of trouble.

So I am starting to get high quite a bit. I am in the eleventh grade and I just buy a brand new Victor 441 single cylinder. This is a nice, powerful bike, and it is brand new.

And I don't know if I was smoking a lot of hash or what I was on, but a friend of mine wants to race me, and he has got a Honda 350, maybe, and I am thinking I am going to kick his ass. And for some reason, I decided to take off my helmet. I can't remember his name.

But anyway, we were on a street in San Fernando Valley. I was 16 years old, probably. And off from the starting line, and we go down the street one way, and it looked pretty even. And we turn around and we are coming the other way, and I think that we are racing the full length of the street again.

He thinks we are over, so he pulls in front of me into the driveway, where he is finishing the race. I slide my motorcycle into a panel truck. Remember, I have no helmet on, brand new motorcycle. I have got about ten miles on it. I slide my 441 Victor right into a panel truck at about between 60 and 70 miles an hour.

I go flying over the truck, do a flip and land on my ass on the front lawn, completely uninjured, but the bike is destroyed. At least the front end is. I have to buy new forks for it, and it was a nightmare. So I guess maybe I could call that a car crash insert or a motorcycle crash insert. I had a lot of motorcycle crashes over the years.

I'm seventeen years old, senior in high school. I have a 1965 Ford Galaxy four door. Ken Olson has a little Datsun pickup truck. We are drunk at about midnight or 1:00 in the morning, driving around the residential streets of the San Fernando Valley in Sepulveda. We decide to have a race. For some reason, I get into races a lot when I am drunk or loaded.

So we get into a straight away race. This would probably be a 20 to 25 mile an hour zone in a very quiet residential zone with lots of children. Of course, it is late at night, and I would say we were going 60 to 80 miles an hour on a straight away.

And we got to a stop sign, and for some reason, I don't know why, I guess we decided the race was over there too, and I hit my brakes and literally did a 360 right in the middle of the street, with cars parked all around me, and somehow avoided hitting any other cars.

Shortly after that, though, we decided to get something to eat and we went to an all night Taco Bell, forgot to put the parking brake on, and when I came back out to my car, my car had run into one of the employee's cars. It had slipped back down the driveway into somebody's car.

I am drunk, of course, and I am trying to unhook the cars. The bumpers are stuck, and I am in the back trying to unhook the bumpers and get out of there before I get noticed. And, of course, the employee comes out of the back door. So these are just a couple of little funny stories that I am relating to you, and I am sure I can come up with a lot more funny stories like that.

Insert number 3. High school. One of the things I used to like to do, especially on the weekends, besides get drunk and go to football games with my friends, was if I could get a date, and a date to me is a bottle of wine and a joint and take a girl up to the hills.

So we used to go to one place called mother's grave. It was a place where supposedly a son had killed his mother with an axe off of Mulholland Drive. We would go up to mother's grave. We would go to Renalde Hills. These are all places around the San Fernando Valley, or up in Topanga Canyon.

We found places in high school that were isolated. They were good places to drink and party. And what I did and what most of the kids did was we would bring our date up to the hills and drink a bottle of Boone's Farm apple wine or strawberry wine or a six pack of beer.

Once in a while, if we were lucky, we would get some good whiskey and mix it with a soft drink and some ice. Then we would get drunk, and if we could get to second or third base, it would be a big deal.

So that is what was going on in high school. So here is just another little high school insert. One thing we used to do every morning, or at least I used to do every morning, when I had my Honda 305, was drive to Winchell's Doughnuts early in the morning.

I used to take a 7:00 a.m. class, so I could get off of school early and then go to work, and I would get what they called school credit for going to work. I would go into school at 7:00, get off at noon and then go to a job.

But I would go to Winchell's Doughnuts at 6:00 a.m. every morning, smoke a joint with some friends in the parking lot, and then eat our doughnuts. And when I am saying it, right now as I am saying, it doesn't sound like a big deal, but that was quite a social event, you know, in those days for a 16, 17 year old kid, you know, for something to do before school.

At that time, I wasn't drinking before school. I normally only drank on the weekends and days off school and once in a while when I was practicing with the band later at night. But anyway, I just thought that was the Winchell's Doughnut insert. I can see myself stuffing my face with a glazed doughnut smoking a joint.

One more little insert right here. Upon graduating from high school, about a week afterwards, I had decided I was going to go live off the land up in Idaho. My friend and I, Dennis Markowitz, took an old '65 Ford pickup truck up there to investigate.

And I had gone to a Jethro Tull concert the night that we were leaving on our vacation and, as usual, I was pretty much loaded out of my mind. So we got in our pickup truck after the concert, and we headed up, I believe, Highway 5 going towards Grapevine, through Mojave. I guess that would have been the 14.

Anyway, I don't remember which highway it is, but we were going to go up Highway 5, I believe all the way to Canada. We were going to go to Canada, or to the top of Idaho, to Sandpoint, Idaho. But about two or three I was taking the first shift. And, unfortunately, I wasn't eating any white crosses at that time.

White crosses are what we called bennys or speed, which helped keep us awake. Anyway, apparently, I fell asleep while I was driving out in the desert. And I heard someone scream, and I woke up, and we were probably 20 feet off the highway out in the middle of some cactus.

And we got the truck stopped and didn't crash, and Dennis didn't let me drive for a couple of days after that. So it was an amazing trip, and I bring it up as an insert, but maybe it could probably be a chapter on its own. my first vacation after high school.

But we drove up through Mammoth and Yosemite. We ended up in Idaho. We drove through Oregon and Washington, ended up camping out up in Sandpoint, Idaho, and met some people living off the land, picking berries and shit. And we camped out for a little while and got eaten by some bugs and said, this isn't for us.

And we hopped back in the truck and we drove, I believe, then to Yosemite, stayed in Yosemite for a while. I loved it up there in Yosemite. And, basically, we just sat around and drank wine and smoked hash and camped out. And had a little problem with some black bears up there, but other than that, everything was pretty cool.

CHAPTER 4

TEENAGE TRIPPING WITH FOLKS AND MORE TROUBLE BREWING

My parents were starting to get pretty mad at me and my lifestyle and sometimes I would stay out late, and my dad would embarrass the heck out of me. I remember a couple of times, one time, he you know, I didn't come home and they went out looking for me, and I was talking to a girl, maybe I was even kissing her. I don't remember. I was about 14 or 15 years old, and I had been drinking, and it was a Saturday night, and all of a sudden, I felt somebody grab me by the ear, and it was my dad, and he grabbed me by the ear and pulled me out of that party.

Boy, I hated his guts. We really started to come apart with each other not long after that. And what happened was I became very, very rebellious, to say the least. After he did that a couple of times, we got in a fistfight one day, and after that, I told him, if he ever touched me again or if he ever came in my room that I would kill him. And we didn't talk after that. I was about 15, 15 and a half years old then.

And they had chained up my motorcycle and you know, I was just getting in lots of trouble, mostly for smoking cigarettes and drinking. And one morning at about 2:00 in the morning, I took a hacksaw to the chain on my motorcycle and I drove off, and I drove about 100 miles north to a little place called Solvang. It is called Buellton. Solvang is like a Dutch village, and there was a horse ranch there and a bowling alley there, and I started bowling there, and I met some people and I got a job on this horse ranch fixing fences and it is called the Flags Up Horse Ranch. It is still there to this day, I think.

Anyway, after working for a few weeks, I saved some money and then I hitchhiked back south to the Los Angeles Airport and bought myself a ticket to Canada and flew to Canada. And, of course, I had a phone number. There was somebody I was going to meet up there, and Immigration wanted that phone. So I gave them the phone number and nobody answered.

And what happened was they said: Look, here is this guy. He has no luggage and he is dressed like a cowboy. I used to wear cowboy boots and a leather jacket, and I am sure it looked pretty funny, you know, a 15 year old kid, chain smoking, dressed like a cowboy. And they found out that there was an all points bulletin, I guess you would call it, looking for me, and they deported me back to California to the juvenile authorities.

And my parents showed up there, and the plan was that they had decided that I should go to foster care, because I was incorrigible, and I was pretty much good with that. That was the way it was going to go. But I started thinking about it, and I said, you know, that is like jail. I don't want to go to jail. I am not that bad.

And so I remember we were I can't remember the whole thing, but we were in a police station or a juvenile hall, someplace, and my parents were there and there were some other authorities there. And the deal they made was that I join a church and I go back to school and I get good grades and then I don't have to go to juvenile hall or a foster home, and I agreed to it, and that was what we did.

CHAPTER 5

BAND, BOOZE AND GETTING HIGH IT ALL COMES TOGETHER

I still wasn't a very good kid and I still got in a lot of trouble, but that was the story. And now I am in eleventh grade, and I started smoking a little bit of marijuana with some people too, and I am growing my hair long, and I want to be a hippy, and, oh, it is kind of a blur. I didn't do too good those last couple of years in high school. I just barely graduated.

I had started a band also. So now I am in a band with Ken Olson and Jeff Basenberg. And I play guitar and I sing and we play rock 'n' roll. We play Jimi Hendrix and Johnny Winters and Janis Joplin and we it was the good times.

By this time, I got a fake ID. I can buy my own beer. And Jeff and Kenny both have older brothers that can buy us booze also. And my parents decide that either I go to college or quit the band or I've got to leave home. And I don't want to leave home, because I am trying to save money to buy instruments and new amplifiers.

So I agree to go to college, and I go to a place called Pierce Junior College and I enroll in about five classes, and within about three weeks, I have dropped out of all of them except for accounting. And across the street from Pierce College is a place called West Valley Occupational School.

And I walk over there, and I am looking in the classes and I see this one class that is all women. And I say: What is this? And they say: That is court reporting, a court reporting class. And my mother had an old stenograph machine. And I say: Well, I will try that. I am going to quit college and I am going to start this court reporting school.

And I did very, very well there. I became it was something that I was just kind of a natural at. I went to the court reporting school in the morning until noon and then I went to a TV shop on Topanga Canyon in Chatsworth, where I worked for about five hours, and then I got off work there and I would go to work at a bookstore next door and worked there until midnight.

So I stayed real busy, and I had a lot of free time in the TV store, because basically all I did was load TVs in people's cars when they showed up to get a TV, and I practiced guitar and I got good on guitar while I was going to court reporting school, when I was about 19, I was at lunch one day and the police, plain clothes police pulled me over for looking suspicious. That was their reason. And they found a little bit of marijuana, and I was just devastated, because I really wanted at that point, I wanted to be a court reporter, and now I get busted for pot, and it was a big deal. I mean, they threw me in jail.

And so I fought the case and I ended up winning that case on an illegal search and seizure, and didn't get arrested again for almost five years.

One little funny after note was, I had turned 18 during this period of time, and this bookstore was next door to the TV store, and I wanted a job at that bookstore, because they paid $2.25 an hour, which was 50 cents more than minimum wage. And when they hired me, they made me take a polygraph test, and I didn't know why, because I walked in the bookstore before and it was just a regular bookstore with magazines and comics and books.

And it turned out that there was a special door in there that you paid to go through and it was all pornographic material on the other side of that door. Anyway, I got a job there, and I worked there from 5:00 to midnight, and that was quite an experience. One of my jobs was to put plastic wrappers on all of the pornographic magazines, and that was a strange time in my life.

What happened when I was working at that bookstore was one night, just about closing time, somebody asked me for help with a magazine. I went down to help them and I looked down and there was a gun pressed up against my balls. And he said: You get in the bathroom. And I said: Yes, sir. And I went in the bathroom. I believe he robbed a few hundred dollars from the cash register and several pornographic reel to reel movies or something like that, and the police showed up. And I decided I didn't want to die, so I quit that job.

I always wanted a chopper, so I saved money from that job and bought one.

Me and my Mom 1974 Triumph 650

And I also had graduated from the court reporting school with a six month scholarship to another court reporting school, because this occupational school only took you through to the secretarial level. So I didn't really want to be a court reporter. I wanted to be a rock star, so I gave away the scholarship, which pissed my parents off to no end. And by this time now, I have bought a Triumph 650 and chopped it, so I am driving around in a chopper and I have got long hair. I am drinking now closer to daily.

I am 18, almost 19 years old, and my direction is I am going to be a rock star. Anyway, I decide, okay, I will go back to this court reporting school. And I go to the court reporting school and there are all girls there, and I am having fun. I have got a girlfriend now too. Her name is Ljubica, and we are in love, but I am playing with the band and I am meeting other girls too, and it was really my downfall, because I loved this girl Ljubica, L j u b i c a. Ljubica was my first love and I have never probably loved anybody the same as I have loved her since.

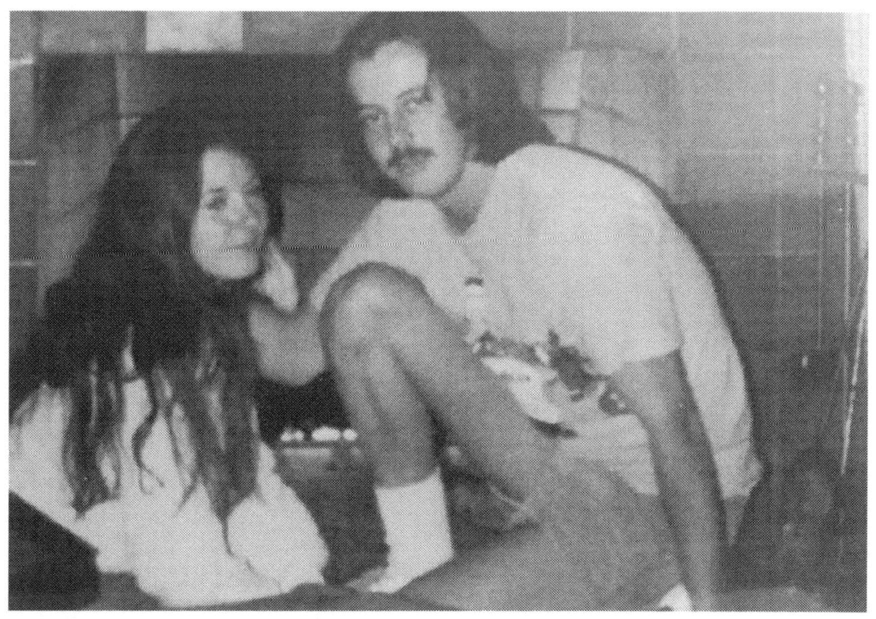

I was 19 years old when I met her and I wanted to marry her. And what happened was I started drinking a lot of hard liquor when I was about 19, and I think she kind of got fed up with it. At one point, we were hiking in Dahunga Canyon and we went back there swimming, and I drank a bunch of tequila, and before the end of the day, I couldn't walk, and Ljubica and her friends had to carry me out of that canyon.

And I could see us, we were drifting further apart, and I just it just crushed me, you know, when she broke up with me and left me for another guy. Really, really crushed me. From the age of 19 on, I never went a day without drinking. I became a whiskey drinker, whiskey and seven. I drank whiskey and seven and I drank beer and I smoked pot. That's what I do.

So I am 19 years old. I am in court reporting school. I have also started a part time job at a court reporting company for a man named Bill Cuff. And the band is practicing every night and looks like it is a good life. It is a good life. Getting high, drinking, playing rock 'n' roll.

And I quit school and I moved into a house with a couple of other musicians. And so that was it. I was going to become a rock 'n' roll star. I moved out of my house. I quit court reporting school and I am going to be a rock star. I am 19 years old and I have got the world by the tail.

Well, that house turned into an absolute nightmare. I think five of us were living there in a four bedroom house, and we played rock 'n' roll every day, and the cops showed up at the house on almost a daily basis for disturbing the peace, and we drank and played rock 'n' roll and drank and played rock 'n' roll, and we had parties and the house just got completely destroyed, and the landlord evicted us, and I moved back home with mom and decided I wanted to go back to court reporting school.

So I went back to court reporting school one more time. And I don't remember the sequence of events, to tell you the truth. There used to be a joke at the court reporting school, where is Ed Fisher? Because I would only show up for the tests. I practiced a lot. I practice on my own a lot at home, and I was good. You know, I got fast on the court reporting machine, and I passed all of the tests. And I used to go to a Mexican restaurant across the street from the school for lunch and get a pitcher of margaritas. And there was always the joke: Where is Ed Fisher? Because I only showed up for the tests. I used to miss a lot of classes. And I quit school again, and I had a job working at a court reporting company. I was making some money translating other people's notes for them and being a secretary.

And I had moved up into a place called Box Canyon, and Box Canyon was not far from the Spahn Ranch, which is where the Manson family had lived at one time, and a lot of the people in Box Canyon were drifters, were breakoffs of the Manson group, and I became friends with a lot of them, and we played music and got high and got drunk.

Left to right, Jeff, Steve, Ken,and Eddie Fisher

Jeff

I decided I wanted to go back to school one more time, because I wasn't making I don't remember why, but anyway, I decided to go back to school and get my court reporting license. I was about 20 years old, and my parents decided they weren't going to help me, because I had quit too many times. And so I said, I will show them. I went back to school on my own, and I pretty much worked full time and went to school full time, and I finished school and got my court reporting license.

And what happened after that was I became a half ass court reporter and a half ass musician, and it was pretty humiliating, because I had to cut my hair to be a court reporter, which I swore I would never do. And the band was pretty much getting sick of me. I was drinking really, really heavily now, and the band was like, you know what? We don't really need you anymore. And it really, really hurt my feelings, and I pretty much spiraled out of control.

I was about 22, 23 years old and, basically, I had gotten kicked out of the band. And I can't remember a lot during that period of time. I was just drinking a lot and I was a court reporter. I used to work in downtown Los

Angeles as a freelance court reporter. Sometimes I worked in the courtrooms and sometimes I worked in depositions. And I hated it. I hated wearing a suit and tie. I hated driving from the mountains of Box Canyon into downtown Los Angeles. I hated looking for parking spots. I hated attorneys and judges and cops, but so there was my double life.

At nighttime, I got drunk and smoked dope and in the daytime, I was a court reporter. So I didn't like my life too much then, and I guess let's see. I am not quite near the end of side one on this tape yet. I will get to this other spot.

I am living up in Box Canyon and I am drunk one night and somebody offered me something to smoke called PCP, or called angel dust. And I smoked that stuff, and later on that night, I woke up and I felt like I was having a heart attack. And I kept drinking to try and I thought maybe, you know, I was having cramps in my chest, and I said, well, if I drink enough, it will to away.

Eventually, I got drunk, but the cramps didn't go away. And what had happened was, I believe, is this angel dust that I smoked created blisters on my lung, and my lung collapsed, and there was a lot of pressure in my chest, and it felt like a heart attack, and I was brought to the hospital and they poked some holes in my chest to release the pressure. Eventually, I wasn't getting any better. The lung wouldn't reinflate, so they operated on me and they took out a piece of the lung and sewed it up. I spent about a month there in the hospital.

I became very religious at that time. I swore to God and to Jesus if they got me through this alive I would never smoke another cigarette or drink another you know, I think when I said, "I will never drink again," I meant hard liquor. But anyway, I said, I am not going to smoke. I am not going to drink. I am going to be good. I am going to go to church. I am going to become athletic again. And I don't know if it lasted for three days or for a week, but I was drinking beer shortly after getting out of that hospital. And before long, I had a girlfriend who smoked, and I started smoking cigarettes again and drinking hard liquor again, and I don't know.

And as I said earlier, I had to go back to church when I was about 15, you know, in order to stay out of juvenile hall, and I began to like that church a lot. We went on a lot of camping trips and stuff. Unfortunately, the vice principal of my high school was also the group leader, and it was a really weird scene, because I was like kind of an outcast, but I made a lot of friends there and I had a lot of fun.

And I was allowed to smoke. I actually had a written permission from my parents to smoke. I was the only kid in my church that was allowed to smoke. Unfortunately, when I was about 17, some of the kids got caught with marijuana on a trip up to Yosemite, and I wasn't one of them. But the word had gotten out that I was a troublemaker in high school and had been in trouble with alcohol and pot before, so the parents all got together and they called a meeting and they said they were going to remove all of their kids from that particular church if I stayed in there. And it was embarrassing for my parents and for me and for everybody else, and so I quit that church then.

It was just kind of a nightmare. And the band didn't want me around either. So I said, I am going to leave Box Canyon and I am going to move up to Tahoe.

One of the reasons I wanted to move to Tahoe is because I knew that Ljubica, the girl that had broke up with me three years prior to that, had moved up there with her fiance, and I thought maybe, you know, I could get them to break up and I will get back with her.

Anyway, I never even saw her the whole time I was up there. I went up there and I got a job as a court reporter and I lived on the North Shore in a place called Incline Village. I had an office in Carson City, and I worked at little one room courthouses in about a 200 mile radius all around Nevada, northern California.

And what would happen is I would go into a town where I was going to be working on a trial for a week or two, and usually there was only one bar in the town. I would get known very quickly, and I would get drunk for a week and work on the trial and leave town.

I have a few stories. I will tell one story real quick. I got stuck in this town about 180 miles east of Carson City, a little one bar town with a wood burning stove in the courthouse. And when the trial was over, a snowstorm hit. It was a bad snowstorm. My car had six feet of snow on top of it. Couldn't move.

So I am in the hotel, and there are no more hotels for anybody, and I meet these two girls in the bar. Actually, they were strippers from Las Vegas, and they needed a room. So I said, well, you guys can stay with me. And one of them says, no, I am going to try to drive out of here. The other one said she would stay with me.

So anyway, this girl stayed with me for a few days, and when the snow finally let up and we could dig the car out, we drove back to Carson City or to Reno. I drove her to an airport, and she was a nice girl. She was a stripper, but she was a nice girl. And I forget what happened. We exchanged phone numbers but we lost touch with each other. Shortly after that, I decided I was going to leave Lake Tahoe. What happened was I was just getting drunk way, way, way too much. One of the reasons I went up there was, I am going to quit getting high and I am going to turn my life around, and I turned it around all right. I was drinking more whiskey than ever.

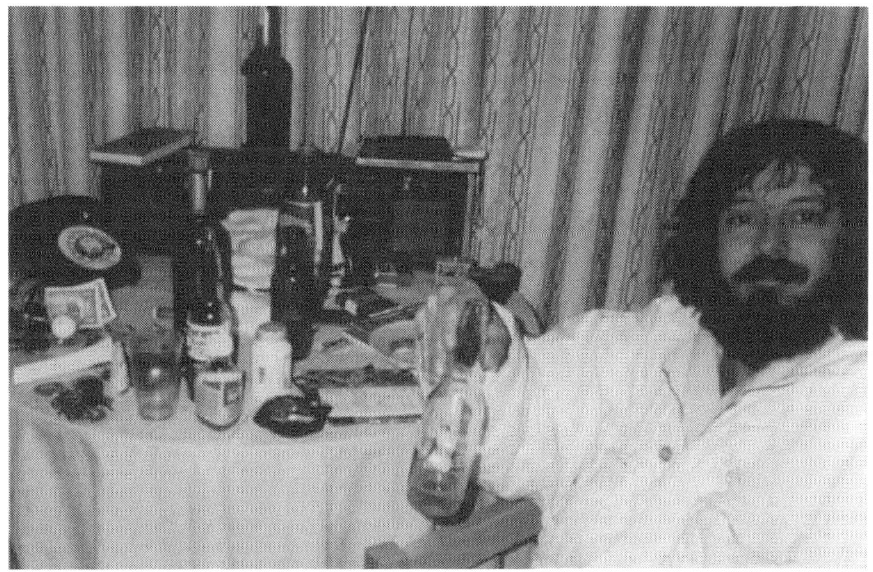

And one of the last jobs I took up there, I had, for some reason, drove off and forgot all of my suits and ties and all of my clothes in this hotel. And I just said, screw it, and I drove back to Los Angeles and back up to Box Canyon to my friend's house and got a job at a court reporting company in Los Angeles again and started all over.

I decided to leave Box Canyon, move up to Lancaster, California and go into the real estate business with my father, and at the same time started my own court reporting company in Lancaster and worked around the Mojave Desert and China Lake and Lancaster and Palmdale.

Chapter 6

THE LONG ROAD HOME

After returning from Tahoe, I move in with I moved back in with Jeff Basenberg for a while. Things aren't really working out. I get a job as a court reporter again in downtown Los Angeles that I hate. I am drinking very heavily. I had a girlfriend, a couple of girlfriends for a short time. I really had a hard time holding girlfriends because of my drinking. Things never really seemed to work out.

And then I left Jeff's house and ended up moving in with Kenny, Ken Olson. And he lived up there near Box Canyon also, a place called Eagle Mountain, and we had a studio in the garage. And even though I wasn't playing with the band anymore, I was allowed to mess around in the studio, and I was still writing some songs and trying to make things work.

Once again, I kind of left a little part out. Before I went back to Jeff's house, after Tahoe, I left Jeff's house. I actually moved into Palmdale with my parents, and I started working for my dad's construction company, and at the same time had a court reporting company up there, and I would travel all the way out to the Mojave and up to China Lake, do depositions and courthouse work. And when I didn't have work with them, I would work on the construction crew, building houses, and it was kind of fun.

I was coming home every weekend to play with the band still back at Topanga Canyon, and eventually I got in a big argument with my dad and we didn't talk for many, many years after that. He said, basically, like either you stay here with the construction company or you go back to your friends. So I went back to my friends.

And at this point, I moved in with Kenny. And that was pretty good for a while, because we all drank the same way. But basically, our lives just revolved around drinking and playing music. Work was just something that was done in between.

I would have a court case or a deposition and I would always end up in a bar at lunchtime, trying to control how much I drank before I went back to work. On the way home, we would all meet some place for happy hour, and then we would go over to Ken's house, where

I lived, and get all revved up and drink some more and work in the studio playing music. And eventually, they didn't even want me there anymore. Things just got really bad.

And I got a new girlfriend named Linda, same name as my lovely sister. By the way, my parents stayed married for 53 years. I started getting along pretty good after I left the house. But anyway, I got involved with this young girl and we were together, off and on, for a few years. And I can't even remember where I moved when I left Kenny's house. Oh, yeah. I moved in with a guy named Jeff Brown.

And I got a house and I had Linda move in with me. And we started arguing a lot, drinking a lot, and eventually she moved out, I moved out, and I moved in with some other kids and she moved in with some other people, and I don't know how it all happened, really, but eventually we got back together and we got married.

And the day of our marriage, I was found in a bar. I was scared to go to the wedding. Her brother found me in a bar about a block from the wedding. It was in North Hollywood at the Little Red Church, it was called, and I was drunk, about 10:00 o'clock in the morning in my tuxedo in this little crappy bar.

And he got me over to the wedding. We got married. And the next day, I don't know, that night, I went out drinking and was playing with my old band and invited everybody over to the hotel where we were at, and it was just a nightmare night. I might have a few pictures of that somewhere. I could insert a couple of pictures from that wedding.

And then we went to Mexico, and I got drunk. I was drinking tequila, and as I recall, I told her I wanted an annulment. But we left Mexico after a few days and we went to Lake Tahoe and went skiing. And I have a couple of pictures of that too. And, you know, we looked like a nice couple, but it just wasn't working.

And what happened was, I moved into a motor home, and we lived in a motor home for a few I don't know, six, three, four, five months, lived in this 28 foot motor home, and I kicked her out one night. And eventually, we got back together again, and then we got an apartment over by Ventura Boulevard.

And at this point, I was starting this closed captioning. I was with research and development. I went from Bill Cuff & Associates, was the name of the company he was the man who had given me my first secretarial job at a court reporting company ten years previously, and we were working on developing a new theory, writing a conflict free theory and trying to get captioning chips built into TVs, working on making instead of having well, don't even type what I just said.

Basically, we were doing a lot of research and development, and it was interesting. I got into transcribing books at one time. I worked with Timothy Leary for a while, also was doing a lot of conventions, traveling around and demonstrating equipment for closed captioning, and started doing closed captioning on a real limited basis, and a little bit of court reporting for a couple of years.

But I don't know. About six, eight, nine months into this marriage thing, it finally all blew up one day, and I kicked her out and regretted it an hour later, and she didn't regret it and she left, and we got an annulment and things got really dark for me.

I was about 28 at the time, not 29 yet, and the next year, it was just a blur. I can't really remember a lot of it. I know I was drunk. Now, I drank every day since I was 19. Up to 19, I was kind of almost I wouldn't say in control, but I wasn't a daily drinker, and I had been a daily drinker since I was 19. I get the shakes now by lunchtime if I don't have a drink.

And at 29, I was just a drunken court reporter and working doing this research and development. But I was really trying I was trying to get my shit together. I was trying to just drink beer during the week and, you know, make it to work every day, and I wanted this closed captioning thing to work.

Chapter 7

Trying to get my shit together.

The research and development years were coming on quick and we were all real excited. We went to a public company. Our company's name was DigiText, and there was four of us and we had some investors. Wang Computers was in with us also and a couple of other companies. And we really thought we were all going to be millionaires.

One day, there was a board meeting, and the board meeting had to do with wanting to send me to treatment to quit drinking. And I wasn't too happy about that. So anyway, like I say, at that time, we were doing some we were doing a lot of conventions. I had been back to Gallaudet College for the Deaf in Washington D.C. to to some demonstrations of our equipment, and I had been to from the San Fernando Valley down to San Diego doing a convention, and then I was sent to the BBC to show them our captioning software, and London to do a convention. I was there for a week or two and then we went to Sweden, Gothenberg and Stockholm where I was on a TV program called "That's Fantastic, and also did a news conference and several demonstrations of the Digitext equipment

While I was in Sweden, I got a job offer from a guy, and it was going to be a great job, I thought. And anyway, my company Digitext didn't want me to go to work for them unless I went through them. This is at a time when I am trying to get my shit together. I was drinking heavily but still had an incredible work ethic and drove me to want to suceed.

Chapter 8

The Boston years 1985 to 1988

So I had my 30th birthday while I was in Sweden. Of course I was drunk already before I even remembered it was my birthday on that night. When I got back to Los Angeles from that trip, they wanted to send me to Boston to WGBH TV to set up some equipment that Boston had bought from DigiText, and I went back there to train some people and help them set up the equipment for a few weeks. And while I was back there, Boston offered me a job.

So I called up my company back in California, and I said, if I can come back there and not go to treatment and you can give me a $10,000 raise, I will come back. And they said, don't bother. Stay in Boston. So I stayed in Boston for three years, and those were three of the best years of my life. It was just absolutely incredible.

I will tell you now, though, that at the time I moved to Boston, I was living in the San Fernando Valley with a guy named Danny Wright. And it was kind of funny, because when

I moved in there, he asked me not to keep any liquor in the kitchen, and I asked him why, and he said: Because my roommate is an alcoholic.

Now, I had been arrested a couple of times in my twenties and been sent to some AA meetings, which I thought were absolutely insane. I was arrested just before I moved into Danny's house. I got evicted from the apartment I was in after my wife left me, and I was arrested on a DUI, and that was kind of a funny story.

I am 29 years old and I am out drinking with some friends and dancing with this girl, and so I told her, I said: You can't drive. You are too messed up. So she gave me her keys and I took her keys. It was a huge rack of keys. And I don't remember a lot that night, but I did get arrested and went to jail, and in the morning, when they were releasing me to Bill Cuff, from Bill Cuff & Associates, they said: Here are your belongings. And they handed me this huge ring of keys. I didn't know where they came from. They were this girl's keys, and those of her live in boyfriend who ran a very successful business with many locks and doors..

These keys went to an office, a big office and a big house, and the guy that owned the office and the house had all of his locks changed, because she thought she had lost her keys. So it doesn't sound so funny when I am saying it, but at the time, it was kind of funny. Anyway, I got out of jail, and that was one more court case I had to fight, and this was the second court case I had fought in my twenties.

Shortly after that is when I moved in with Danny Wright. And anyway, getting back to that, he said: Don't bring any booze in the house. And Danny and I used to go out drinking a lot, and I would come home and his other roommate would be eating candy, watching TV. And it turned out and I didn't know what a sponsor was. It turned out that Danny went to Alcoholics Anonymous, and this guy that was living with him was his sponsor, and I was blowing their whole scene, because I am living with Danny and I am drinking up a storm and Danny is going out drinking with me and going to AA in between and trying to get sober, and I went to a couple of AA meetings with him and I didn't like it.

So when this opportunity came up for me to move to Boston, I said, it is time to go. By the way, Danny's sponsor moved out. Danny couldn't take it or whatever his name was.

Danny's sponsor had to leave the house. He couldn't handle living with me. And those were some crazy times.

What happened was, I came back from Boston after a couple of weeks, packed up everything I could and shipped it to Boston, found a place to live back there and went to work at WBGH TV, where I stayed for three years.

It was really the beginning of the real time closed captioning in 1984, '85. And my girlfriend that I did get engaged with there was my supervisor at the TV station. Shortly after I moved to Boston, the man I had met in Sweden came over to meet me, and was trying to hire me to move to Sweden.. My head was spinning.

So in 1984, at the end of '84, after I was asked to go to treatment, just before I was supposed to go to treatment for alcoholism, I needed to go to first I went to London to do a demonstration with the BBC on the captioning, and stayed drunk the whole time I was there, and shortly after that, I went to Gallaudet College in Washington, D.C. And then in January of 1985, I went to Sweden on a very important business trip and met with the Prime Minister of Social Affairs, I believe, and did quite a few demonstrations and a news conference. I was on a TV showed called "That's Fantastik" with a K in Sweden demonstrating closed captioning equipment, and they offered me a job, as I mentioned before.

Shortly after that, after I went back to L.A., they needed me to fly out to Boston. I had been to Boston about three or four months earlier to close caption the Miss America Pageant in 1984, and that was the first time it had ever been closed captioned. I close captioned it for WGBH TV, and WGBH ended up buying our equipment from DigiText, and I went out there to help them set up the equipment and train some people.

I was supposed to stay for three weeks, and as I mentioned earlier, I ended up I came back to Los Angeles for about one week and packed up and left and went back to Boston, because of a disagreement that I had with the DigiText company in Los Angeles.

So I ended up moving to Boston, and it was a real good move for me. I don't know how good it was for the TV station. What happened was they made me feel real important, because at the time, there were only maybe half a dozen of us doing what I did in the real time closed captioning world, and I was indispensable, which is kind of dangerous. We had three people there that were training. Two of them never made it through the training. The other one took about six months, almost a year. And I was, like I said, very indispensable to WGBH at that time.

And I believe my working hours were, I had I was supposed to be there from about, oh, I think noon or 1:00 until 10:30 or 11:00 at night. And the way it would usually work is, I would come in at noon and I would study for about an hour and work with some people for a while and then I would take off and go on a two or three hour lunch. I might spend it at the bar. I might spend it at the golf course.

I would come back, and then I would have a couple of shows to do between 4:00 and 7:00 o'clock at night, and then I would leave. I would go to the bar for about two hours down the street, until about 9:00 o'clock, and then I would come back to the TV station. I would have a show at 10:00 o'clock. I would finish that show at 10:30, and then I would go out to some other bars, where some friends of mine were playing music, and hang out until closing time.

What else happened while I was there

was, I had been not playing music for a long time. I had been very depressed about playing music since I had been kicked out of the band in my late twenties, and I brought a guitar out there with me and I bought a new guitar while I was in Boston, and I went to a real good music teacher and I started learning how to play old Texas, Louisiana blues. And within a few months, I had hooked up with a couple of people in Boston and had started playing open mikes and then sitting in with bands all around Boston. So three or four nights a week, I was out until 2:00 in the morning playing with other bands and getting drunk all night, and I just thought it was a great life. I really did.

I ended up meeting a couple of different women. One of them happened to be my supervisor. She was married, but that didn't stop us from having an affair, unfortunately for her. Her husband threatened to kill me, but it ended up, they got a divorce.

And anyway, life went on in Boston for a while. I had a good time there for a couple of years and things started going downhill. I was getting really tired of the cold weather. And what happened was, that led to me leaving Boston was, I got jealous of somebody. After I had a couple of affairs and had cheated on my then fiance, who was also my supervisor, she went out with somebody else who worked at the TV station.

I got very jealous. I called up the TV station and got a hold of him and threatened to kill him. And when I went down to the TV station, my security card didn't work. I couldn't get in. They had decided they were going to fire me. So I got a hold of my at that time, I was in a union. So, basically, when you are in a union, you can't get fired.

So anyway, basically, what happened was, we all got together, and they wanted to fire me, and I came forward with some allegations that were not allegations; they were true facts of a lot of things I knew about senior people that were in the TV station, and I won't go into specifics, but they had to do with sexual allegations, sexual harassments and drug use that was taking place on the premises of the TV station, which was on Harvard campus.

And so what they did was, they gave me six months of paid leave and the most brilliant resume that you could imagine. I mean, they recommended me as the most highly prized closed captioner in the United States and that any company that was able to hire me would be very lucky. They gave me a very, very good recommendation.

I was going to go to the Closed Captioning Institute, NCI, National Captioning Institute in Washington, D.C. I went down there for an interview and stayed in Georgetown for a few days and, of course, I was drunk the whole time I was there, and I got accepted for a job there at the National Captioning Institute.

But I thought, before I take this job, I want to go back out to the West Coast and see what is going on out there. So I came to San Diego, and the only thing they had available here for me was a little part time job that didn't pay much money. But it was February, I believe, January or February, and we had our interview at a place called The Trident in Cardiff by the Sea, right on the ocean. And it was about 75 or 80 degrees, and dolphins were jumping out in the water, and I had just come from the East Coast. And I said in my mind, I was thinking, I don't care what the money is or what the hours are. This is where I want to live for the rest of my life, and I moved to San Diego.

And so shortly after that, the San Diego years started, but the Boston years weren't really over. I had a lot of stuff to move back here. I had a fiance that things ended really, really badly with us. And I was really in love with her, and as she put it, she felt like she had wasted three years with me.

The move back here was not easy. I had established an entire life in Boston and I had a lot of things to move back here. And let's see. What else? Well, it was hard leaving all of my friends. That was my new life, you know. I didn't want to leave all of my friends in Boston, but I was really the cold was killing me.

So before I had left Boston, I went down to Key West for about a week, just to get out of the cold, and that was quite an adventure too. Also we went snow skiing and fishing up at Lake Winnipesaukee. I took a lot of nice little vacations up in New England and into Maine and Vermont, New Hampshire. And so it was a very interesting, good part of my life, living in Boston and traveling around up there, and they made me feel wanted.

Dad and my fiance

Another thing that happened while I was there was, I ended up selling all I was a stockholder in DigiText Corporation still back in Los Angeles, and I ended up selling all of my stock and came into quite a bit of money. So now I have got a lot of money, which is dangerous for a guy like me, and I also have six months' salary, so I have a paycheck coming in every two weeks for the next six months, whether I work or not.

And so when I left Boston, before my job wasn't going to start for four months, so I got a four month vacation between January and May, I think, in San Diego, so I spent a few weeks up in Lake Tahoe, just getting plastered out of my mind and snow skiing and sleazing around, you might say. And from there, I left and went to Cabo San Lucas. I went down to Cabo San Lucas and went fishing for about a week or so.

And then I went up to San Diego and found myself a place to live and settled in, and that's where the San Diego years start, and I have plenty of pictures in San Diego. I have been in San Diego for most of the last from about 1988 to the present, which is now 2012, as we speak, and there were a few different moves in between, but a whole new life started in San Diego. It looked like it was going to start out really good, and things changed real quick. My drinking was horrible, and I was missing my girlfriend terribly, so I was very depressed and lonely. That was kind of a sad thing. And then I got involved in a drug called cocaine, which didn't help things either.

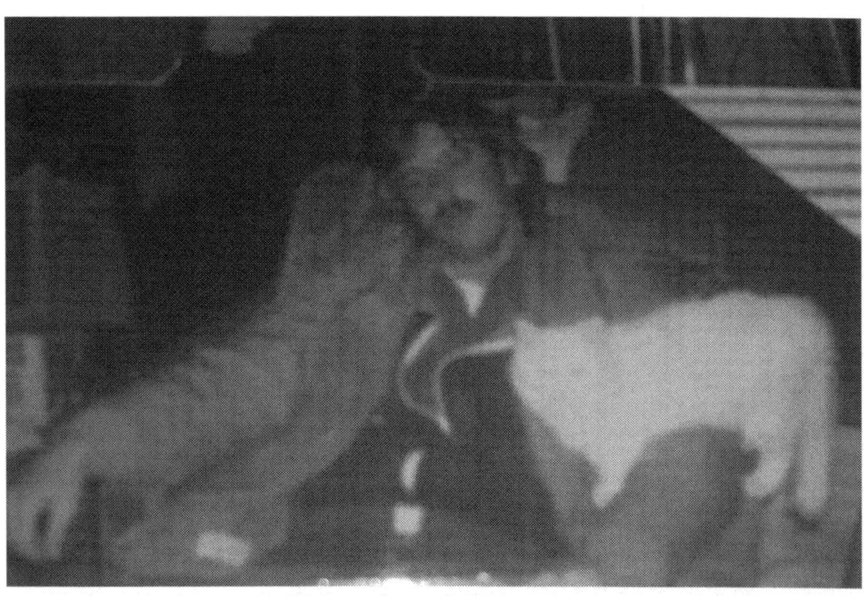

Drunk with my cat

Chapter 9

The arrest years

So at seven years old, as I said before, I get in trouble for the arson, with the fire chief, but there is no arrest. Also at seven years old, I run away from home and I get caught shoplifting and I am brought home in a police car. I wouldn't say it was an arrest, but I was in a police car.

At eleven years old, I am caught shoplifting again. I had been shoplifting for the entire time, for about four or five years, and I finally got caught. So here I am. Shoplifting. And I get brought into the Van Nuys police station. And I got in a lot of trouble for that one. Now I quit shoplifting. I am not shoplifting anymore. I am a good kid. I have got a paper route and I am being good. I am getting good grades in school.

And eventually, as I start drinking, when I am 13, I start getting in trouble again. And at 15, I run away from home and I go to Canada and I get arrested and brought into juvenile hall for that one. That was a big deal. And I think I mentioned that before.

So then we move in to about six month later. I am arrested for a myriad of things. I have a passenger on a motorcycle. I am arrested for high speed pursuit, resisting arrest, driving under the influence, and also, they found these little purple pills. I think Jimi Hendrix used to call them purple haze. They were LSD. And LSD was thrown from the back of my motorcycle from a passenger. Again, at 19, I am arrested for looking suspicious in an area that had been burglarized, and in that case, I beat that case. They found a roach in my car.

I am arrested again at 23 or 24. I am living in a house where they find 28 pounds of homegrown marijuana. That case, I end up going to aversion and going to meetings.

I am arrested again for drunk driving, and it was reduced to reckless driving at the age of 28 or 29. I can't remember. In between these times, I probably have 50 run ins with the law for disturbing the peace, of which I am never arrested for. Again, I am arrested at age 32 or 33 for driving under the influence and open container in Boston, Massachusetts.

Again, I am arrested in San Diego at 38 or 39 for driving under the influence. I believe they found cocaine on me at that time too, and that became a felony conviction. Again, I am arrested the same year for another driving under the influence as I am driving into a parking lot of a bar, and that was an absolute nightmare.

So that kind of concludes the arrests for the time. There were a lot of other problems with the police, and I was on probation probably for a total of ten years between the ages of 19 and 40, maybe a lot more years. I can't remember.

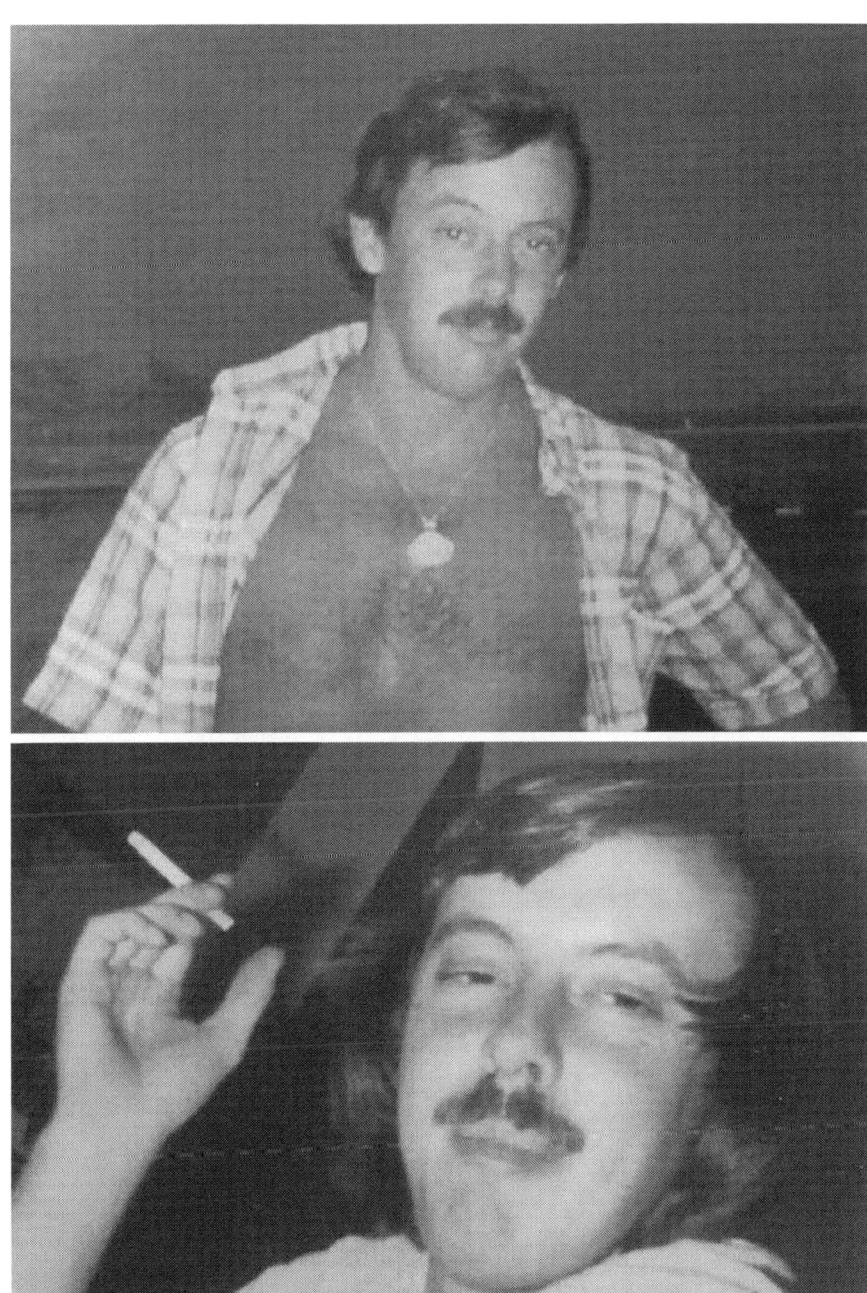

Chapter 10

The Camping years

The camping years, I began at about 15 or 16 driving up to the mountains with my friend, Randy Semard, and we would just hike back into the mountains for a night, you know, bring a bunch of beer or wine with us and some hash and stay back in the hills for a day or two.

At about 17, I started going to Yosemite on a very regular basis, at least once a month, and I really loved it, and those were what I would call the wine and hash years. I used to really enjoy smoking a lot of hash and drinking a lot of wine and camping out up in Yosemite and hiking around the mountains. Also, you will see a lot of hallucinogenics at that particular time in my life. So that was a lot of fun and I enjoyed that quite a bit, and I wasn't getting in any particular trouble at that time.

One time we were camping in a campground in Big Sur, California, absolutely gorgeous. Now, remember, this is 1972. I hiked way back up in the mountains, and I went past some signs that said no trespassing, and it was just really interesting.

I was scared to look through the bushes, but there was an incredible musician playing music and singing back there, and talking to the birds, but I couldn't peek around the bushes because I wasn't supposed to be there.

Anyway, as I am coming back down the path and I am way up in the mountains I hear some screaming, what I think is screaming. And I dodged down behind a rock, and I look around the rock, and I see a woman naked on top of a man. She is having an orgasm and she is screwing the heck out of him. Now, embarrassing enough to say as it is, up to this point, I had had several sexual experiences, but technically, I was still a virgin, so I am watching people have sex for the first time in my life. Oh, my God. Looking back on it, it was shocking, is what it was. And I probably should draw like an animated picture of it.

The guy still had his pants down to his ankles with his shoes on and the girl was naked on top of him and they were next to a stream. It was just an idyllic situation and it turned out that they were camping right next to me. So it was almost surreal.

Also, I used to go camping up at a place called Kern River, and I went up there with Jeff and Kenny and our girlfriends, and we had a lot of fun up there. And one particular day I remember on this particular trip was, I am floating down the river on a perfect day. It is about 85 degrees. There is not a cloud in the sky. I was smoking a joint and I have a half a gallon bottle of wine in my hand. I think it was Spanada. And it just seemed like life was perfect. I thought if there was a heaven, this would be it, and I searched for that day again for the next 23 years. That day never was recreated again.

So anyway, I just thought that was kind of funny how wonderful I thought life was at that particular time at age 19 or 20, floating down the river with a bottle of wine and a joint. I just thought life could never be better than that.

I just loved Yosemite, and I camped out there many, many times. Originally, I went there as a young boy with my family, when they still had what they called the fire falls. And when you went up to upper Yosemite, they had an area where they would build a big campfire, and at one point, somebody would kick the fire off with their boot, but they ended up using it was like a big broom made out of steel, and they would push the fire off the cliff, so if you were down below, you could see the fire falls. It was called the fire falls. The fire falls would go down the cliff, and if you were up at the top where we were, you would watch it go down the cliff. It was kind of cool. And they don't do that anymore. Things change over the years.

I did start going camping, like I said, with my friend on my motorcycle, and we would go up to the San Bernadino mountains and Ojai, and some places like that, but also and I am going to do a chapter called the church years.

At one point when I rejoined thc church, when I was 16, after my runaway experience and I had to join the church, I really enjoyed it, and I was part of the youth group, and I think it was a Methodist church. And one of the places we went camping the first year was Yosemite, and it was absolutely wonderful.

We spent a week up there, not the whole week in Yosemite, but it was really gorgeous and I really felt inspired spiritually at that time, and I was really happy to be a part of that group, and I enjoyed the church at that time. The next year and there was a girl, of course, I liked there too, so that made it easier. And I was playing music with some of the guys there and learning acoustic songs and singing and having fun. The next year, we went to Sedona, and that was equally impressive. Just had an absolutely wonderful time camping out all around Arizona and Sedona, the Grand Canyon.

Later in my twenties, we started going in motor homes or in hotels, and we would go to Big Bear and Mammoth and Tahoe, to Lake Mead, learned how to snow ski and water ski, and just had some wild, drunken trips. We had a lot of fun. Me and Jeff and Kenny would all bring our guitars with us wherever we went, whether it was snow skiing or water skiing, or wherever we went, we would have campfires or go to the local bar and become a trio and start playing songs and meet women and get drunk and have fun. And that was what we did.

And then I went on a couple I went on my first back on a long backpacking trip with my church also when I was 17, and I enjoyed that so much that later on, in my early twenties, I did the same thing with my girlfriend and another couple. And then later, I was probably about 27 or 28, I went with a girl I was living with, Linda. Her name was Linda Guidry, and that was the girl that I ended up marrying and asking for an annulment. I don't even remember if I told that story yet, but I will probably write a chapter called "The girlfriend and fiance years," because I had a lot of different girlfriends over the years and a lot of heartache.

But we went backpacking, and it was kind of funny, because I was addicted to alcohol at that time, and so I said, well, I will just bring like five half pints of vodka and some Tang with me, and some joints, and that should get me by for a week. And we got back up in the mountains, and I don't remember if it was four days or if it was five days but, of course, I ran out of booze.

And that night, I was saying, we can't stay up here any longer, hon. We have got to go back to base camp. We have to find a store that sells liquor. So the next morning, we hiked down, and it took all day to get down, and by the evening, the camp store was just closing, and I begged them to stay open, and they stayed open and I couldn't find hardly any booze in there. All they had was some champagne. So I said, okay, I will take a bottle of champagne.

And I got it back to the campsite, and before I could even open it, I don't know what I did wrong, but the whole thing exploded and I lost almost all of it. It was just it just terrified me. I was so upset. I ran back to the store. They had already locked it up, and I don't remember if I paid them extra or I yelled at them or if I was really nice or what. I just don't remember, but I did get them to open it back up and sell me a box of wine or a tinfoil bag of wine, I think it was. I don't know if it was a quart or a half gallon or what it was, but it was something that had alcohol content, and it was enough to get me by. So that was kind of a funny story.

And that was not the last time I went camping, but one of the last times. I camped out a couple more times with Linda out at a place called Lake Cuyamaca, east of San Diego, and that was really wonderful. Then another time I went there with Linda and Bill Cuff and his wife, who I am still in touch with to this day. He was one of my first employers, and I probably should write a chapter about that too, Bill Cuff & Associates, first court reporting company I worked for. So I went camping with them.

And I think that is about the end of the camping years. After that, it was always pretty much in hotels. I will tell one funny story. Me and Kenny, when we were about 23 or 24, we took his motor home up to Mammoth Mountain, and I brought I had two dogs, two German shepherds at the time, Bobo and Chow. And Bobo was a really big dog.

Buy anyway, we took them with us, and we would keep them in the camper, and they loved the snow, but we had to leave them in the motor home while we were skiing. And one day, we were taking the lift up Mammoth Mountain from the parking lot, and I heard people yelling and laughing, and I looked down and there was Bobo and Chow running up the mountain following our chairs up the mountain, and we couldn't get them off the mountain for the rest of the day. Nobody could catch them, and they hung out on the mountain that day, just running up and down the mountain in the snow. They just absolutely loved it. They were those two dogs were a lot of trouble for a long time, and that's a story in itself also, Bobo and Chow. Those are the only two dogs I ever had in my life, and I really loved them.

Chapter 11

The Church Years

I was raised in church. I went to church from the time I was a small child, to Sunday school, to Lutheran school, and I went to a Lutheran kindergarten and a Lutheran first grade, and I believe I skipped the second half of the first grade or the first half of the second grade. I was considered gifted, and so I skipped half a grade, and so I was always younger than everybody else in my grade.

And one of the things I remember is, for one thing, I liked it. I enjoyed my church. I don't know why, but I did enjoy it. I enjoyed my school. I remember getting paddled a lot. They used a big, wooden paddle, and either the teacher would use it or the principal. You would get sent to the principal's office and use it.

And looking back on it, people would say, wasn't that abusive? And the thing was, I always knew when I was going to get pretty much knew when I was going to get swatted with this paddle, that I had done something wrong, so at the time, I didn't consider it abusive. I just considered it punishment for doing something wrong, and I did a lot of wrong things all my life, and I always knew there would be punishment, you know, that I would have to pay for it.

I never got punished with paddling in the public elementary school. I went to public elementary school in the fifth and sixth grade, and I really liked it, because I got to go with my friends. I did get paddled at home with wooden paddles and belts on a fairly regular basis, and I always knew when it was going to happen. I mean, I broke rules and I got paddled for it, and that was just the deal. They even carried a paddle in the glove box of the car, and when I didn't follow the rules, they pulled over the car and they hit me with the paddle.

So that is just the way it was, and I accept it and I don't look back on it as my parents being abusive. I look back at them as being strict disciplinarians. So right or wrong, that's the way it was, and I know my parents loved me and that I was a hard kid to raise. I mean, I just they were besides themselves with me. They really were.

And in junior high, they did the same

thing. I had shop teachers. My electric shop teacher used the paddle on me. My PE teacher used the paddle on me. The vice principal of the school used the paddle on me. I was expelled for smoking in junior high a couple of times in the fifth grade, in public school, I got expelled. A friend gave me a deck of playing cards from Tijuana that were pornographic. They had pictures of women and men doing pornographic things and I was showing some I was showing them to some of the fellow classmates. I wasn't even you know, they were kind of shocking, and I got caught and I got expelled for a week, along with the kid that gave me those cards.

High school, same thing. I got paddled on a fairly regular basis from the vice principal and also from the physical education teachers. And I got caught doing a lot of wrong things, besides ditching school and being tardy and smoking and I can't remember what else, but I wasn't the best student.

So anyway, we are still in the church years. So after my Lutheran school, after we graduated, I still kept going to Lutheran I went to Lutheran school every day, and I went to church on Sundays. And then after I joined the public school, I had a friend, Jeff Basenberg, who was a Lutheran also, so I went to his Lutheran church, and that's where Pam and Barbara Wetzel went, so I was happy about that, those twin girls, and I loved Barbara Wetzel, I think.

And we did camping trips and stuff too, so that was a lot of fun, and I stayed in that church all the way through seventh or eighth grade. I went through confirmation. And about the time I started drinking, probably about eighth grade, about 13, about the same time, I think, I quit going to the church, and then like I said, after my runaway experience and so forth, when I was about 15, just maybe before my 16th birthday, I rejoined the Methodist Church.

And because of a bad experience where I got blamed for other kids smoking marijuana on a camping trip and their parents wanted to withdraw their children from the church as long as I was a member, that gave me a really bad taste. And I really liked the kids in that church, and I think they gave me almost a lifelong resentment towards the church. Not really, but I didn't go back to church until after the hospital experience, where I almost died, they cut out a piece of my lung, and I started writing

Gospel songs and reading the Bible.

I was 23 at that time. It was the spring of 1978. When I got out of the hospital, I started going to church again, and that didn't last very long either. And so I basically never went to church again until going to visit my mom up in Oregon in my late thirties no, I guess it would be my forties, my early forties. And currently today, I go to a church called the Seaside Center for Spiritual Living. I have a garden, a vegetable garden that I grow there, and they have a really good band, and a lot of the people there are in recovery from alcoholism or drug addiction, such as myself. I am also an alcoholic. So I find it to be a pretty acceptable place to go, and they don't ram anything down my throat that I can't accept.

So those are my church years, I guess, and I look back on most of them very fondly, and I am sorry things worked out the way they did. Who knows what would have happened if things had gone just a little bit different and anyway. I am not going to reflect on that too much.

Chapter 12

The Box Canyon years

I am going to quickly do the Box Canyon years. I moved to Box Canyon with Jeff Basenberg in 1976. I had started court reporting and we lived up there, and one of the things I loved about Box Canyon is and I am going to write about the work ethic years.

I worked in the early seventies, 1970, '71, '72, I worked up in Box Canyon, Santa Susana Pass for some real estate people and also for the fire department. And I was even quote, unquote awarded, given an award for the fight against drug abuse and helping preserve the environment, signed by President Nixon. I thought it was pretty funny. It was awarded to me by Mayor Tom Bradley at the convention center in Santa Monica after I graduated from high school.

And I worked up in those mountains, and those were the same mountains, Santa Susana Pass, that Charles Manson and his family lived in. They lived at the Spahn Ranch right off of Santa Susana Pass Road, and it intersected with Box Canyon. And I knew there were some crazy people up there.

Most of the people that lived with the Manson family had no idea what Manson was doing. They were just fun loving hippies getting high and drinking and eating acid and walking around the mountains. And I got to know some of them later on in the later seventies.

But I just always loved that area. I loved those hills. I felt removed from the San Fernando Valley. I felt removed from the city. And I had always kind of hated the city, even though I worked as a court reporter in downtown Los Angeles. So we moved up into Box Canyon and we hung out with a lot of strange people up there.

There was one place called The Love Fountain, that had been an old religious sect. There was a building on a creek back there, and a lot of hippies lived up there, and also some of the old members of the Manson family lived up there.

And there was a guy named Richard Margolen who lived up there, and all of the houses were funky, you know, and there was a creek up there and there was we played music up there. Our band played up there. Our band's name was Brain Damage. And there was another band up there called The Oily Scarf Wino Band.

And we had a lot of fun up there. We used to play a game called mumbly plunger. There was even a book written for it with rules. It was played with toilet plungers, and you would put quarters down or dollars down and try and cover the coin or the dollar with the mumbly plunger from ten mumbly plunger links, 20 or 30 feet, and you would flip the plunger around and it would land on an area and stick. And it was a game that while high on LSD and wine could be played for hours.

We hiked all over those mountains and had a lot of fun up there. And there were a lot of people. Dotty lived up there. Dotty lived across the street from us. She fell down in the creek drunk and died. And Dickie, the deaf genius, lived across the street. He built all kinds of absolutely eccentric motorcycles, three wheelers, electronic things. He worked for I can't remember a big airplane company where he helped build electronic circuit boards and stuff for them. And he was deaf, but somehow he could play piano and tuba, and he was part of

The Oily Scarf Wino Band. He died on his motorcycle pulling out of his driveway. A car came around the corner in Box Canyon and hit him.

Another guy up there hung himself. A lot of strange things happened up in Box Canyon. The son of a famous architect, his name eludes me now. He was a very, very famous architect, but his son lived up there at one time and crashed his Porsche up in those mountains and had an incident with a machine gun and so forth. And there was just a lot of crazy stuff that went around down there. There was a lot of LSD, a lot of wine, a lot of sex.

And I lived up there until I was about 24, until I went to Lake Tahoe, and I came back from Tahoe and stayed there for a little while longer, and then I moved out to Palmdale. And that's already in the story.

But the funny thing is, Jeff Basenberg who I originally bought that house with him. I had a lease option to buy. His father put up the money for us. I think we paid $25,000 or $30,000 for it. It is on an acre with a stream in the backyard, a gorgeous old house built in 1929 by a man named Ed Secker.

And Jeff still lives there to this day. It is now August 2012. So it is 36 years later, and Jeff has married and has a couple of children, and he still lives in that house up in Box Canyon, at 191 Box Canyon Road. Still has the same phone number that we had at that time.

chapter 13

The Work Ethics

Even though I was a drunk and a pothead, I worked. And I started working when I was a little kid, eight, nine, ten years old, helping my dad out on construction sites. He built an apartment building in North Ridge and he owned another apartment in Van Nuys, California, near the Van Nuys police station. And one of my jobs, eventually, was helping clean out apartments when people moved out. And eventually, I became the carpet cleaner and the interior painter, and I did that regularly on the weekends. And when I was eleven or twelve years old, I got a paper route, and one paper route wasn't enough, so I got two paper routes.

And then at the same time I had the paper routes, eleven, twelve, thirteen, at the age of about thirteen or fourteen, I started selling flowers on the street corners on the weekend. So I sold flowers on the street corners, I had the paper routes, and I worked for my dad also.

And eventually, I quit the paper routes and the flowers, because it was I was making more money working for my dad. And then I said, I don't want to work for my dad exclusively, so I had cards made up, and I started a business called Ed Fisher's Carpet Cleaning and Interior Painting. And I had 1,000 cards made up and I handed them out, and I started getting jobs doing carpet cleaning and interior painting. And at the same time, I had also gotten a reputation up there in Box Canyon, Santa Susana Pass, by the time I was 17 or 18, and I had started doing repair work around some of the ranches up there.

And those were good years. I was driving my Honda 305, and I also had an old '65 Ford Galaxy that I drove around, and I repaired fences and sawed trees and hoed weeds and did interior painting and carpet shampooing. And eventually, I even painted the exterior of a few houses for my father out in Palmdale, when he was buying old foreclosures up in the Palmdale area.

Then as I started court reporting school, I worked at the TV shop. At one point, I was going to court reporting college four hours a day, I was working at the TV shop for four hours a day, from 1:00 to 5:00, and went straight from the TV shop next door to a book store and worked there from 5:00 to midnight. I worked at the TV shop five days a week, I worked at the bookstore six days a week, and I went to school five days a week, and I practiced my guitar while I was at the TV store, and then when I finished work at midnight, I would go practice with my band.

So I had a very good work ethic, even though I smoked a lot of dope and drank a lot. And then at 19, while I was in court reporting school, I started working as a secretary at Bill Cuff & Associates. That was a court reporting agency in Van Nuys. It was close to the Van Nuys apartment buildings and the police station, unfortunately. And so I worked for Bill Cuff & Associates as a secretary, and I was still doing a little bit of work for my dad managing, taking care of his apartment there at Van Nuys.

And I started Merit College of Court Reporting, which was also on Victory Boulevard in Van Nuys. And then I started to become a note reader and I started reading notes for several different court reporters and became very proficient at several different court reporting theories.

And after I finished school and I started working at Bill Cuff & Associates as a court reporter, not long after that, by 1978, I was on the Baron computer system, and we had Jerry Leffler and Bill Cuff and myself had decided we were going to develop a real time theory, and eventually we wrote the DigiText theory together. It was Jerry Leffler's idea, and I had a lot of input in it also, and we came up with this conflict free theory that we could use to do real time writing.

And at the same time, by about 1980, '81 well, 1980, we had, I believe, the Olympics in Los Angeles, and they were right near our office in Santa Monica, a lot of them at UCLA. And they were trying to do real time closed captioning at that time, and it looked horrible. The National Captioning Institute was doing it, and so we said, we are going to get in on that.

And one of the problems with captioning was they didn't have the TVs didn't have closed caption chips in them. You had to buy a special box from Sears & Roebuck for $400 or $500 and hook it up to your TV. So not too many people even had the capability of watching closed captions, and so not only did we help innovate the real time closed captioning industry with DigiText, we developed real time chips to be put in TVs. We lobbied the government, and as a direct result of DigiText, these little chips were developed and put in every TV in the United States, and they were required to be in every TV by a certain year, more and more of them were put in, and now every TV in the United States has closed captioning chips in it.

I was very, very involved in this research and development, and I was happy, because while I was doing the research and development I didn't have to do as much court reporting, and I had always hated court reporting. And I would like to say that I had the same work ethic as a court reporter as I had as an interior painter and carpet shampooer, but I didn't, because I really hated it, but I will say that when I set up my schedules, I met my schedules. I never missed a day of work, no matter how much I was drinking or how much I was partying.

I drove from the mountains of Box Canyon into downtown Los Angeles and worked mostly in the downtown court system, and I worked in superior court, I worked in juvenile court, I worked in arbitrations, I worked in Civil Service, and I did a lot of depositions, mostly up and down Wilshire Boulevard.

And then at age 26, 27, we started getting really that would have been the early eighties, we got very involved in this research and development, and we sold stock and got involved with Wang, which was an important company at that time, and we started building our own computers and developing this theory, and we started doing a lot of medical transcription and we started to do closed captioning for the hearing impaired, and it was it was a very important age at that time, 27, 28, 29.

I was involved in doing conventions and doing shows for people, and I was very good, and the company valued me, and even though I was a drunk, I was very good at what I did, and I worked really hard with developing the closed captioning, the research and development and training other people.

I really, really did work hard at it. And even though I took a lot of long lunches and came back from lunch drunk, I worked as hard as anybody ever worked in that company. And that was a story I believe I told you already of how I ended up, they wanted me to go to treatment and I ended up going to Boston.

And over the years, my work ethic has changed, but I still always enjoyed working and always enjoyed having a job, and after I worked in Boston for a few years, I worked here in San Diego at I don't remember the name of the captioning Media Captioning. I worked with them and helped them start their company and then worked I had some other odd jobs working at a gas station and doing landscaping and then eventually at a pottery shop, and then I worked at before the pottery shop, I worked, went back up to San Fernando Valley and worked at Kenny Olson's machine shop, and then eventually I went to Vitac Captioning back in Pittsburgh, before I came back to San Diego and got sober and eventually started my own captioning business.

So those are the work ethic years, and now we will get to the San Diego years, where I moved in January of 1988. Yes. January of 1988. I moved here after three years in Boston. Here we go, after this.

Chapter 14

The San Diego years

Okay. So I come to San Diego on a job interview in January of 1988, and the dolphins are jumping and the sun is out, and I said, I am coming back to southern California. I am not staying on the East Coast and I am not going to work in Washington, D.C. at the National Captioning Institute, even though I told them I probably would.

So I went back to Boston, packed all of my things, and I UPSed everything I could, that I couldn't fit on a plane. I had my entire life back there, and I had everything stored for me in a storage place back there by my new employers.

And I came back and I stayed in a hotel for a few weeks, and I found a little two bedroom cottage on the back of an acre in Solana Beach with an ocean view. It was about three blocks from the beach and one block from a bar and one block from a liquor store. It was just perfect.

And I grew marijuana on the property, and I also had an indoor marijuana setup, and I had five months off work, because they hadn't opened up the new office yet in Carlsbad. So basically, all I did was grow vegetables and pot and get high, drink, hang out at the bar, hang out at the bench, and life was just wonderful.

I just really thought things couldn't get any better. And then I had to start working, and I had to work for one hour a day. I was closed captioning and I had one newscast from 5:00 to 6:00 o'clock every day.

By the way, when I was in Los Angeles, before I went back to Boston, I was interviewed on a TV station for this, because closed captioning was such a new thing. And then in Boston also, in 1985, I was interviewed. And they claimed in the interview, and I have the videotape, that I was the first person in the country to real time close caption a local live newscast. There had been some national newscasts, I guess, captioned, but nothing local.

So now I am in San Diego, and Channel 8, KFMB, and Channel 10, KABC, both interview me at my place of work also. Another point of reference was, from the age of 20 to 30, I cut my hair to start court reporting when I was 20, 21, and I always wanted to grow my hair long, and every time my hair started to get long, they made me get it cut.

So at one point, I just got a regular boy's haircut, and I have my passport I got when I was 29 years old where I have a regular boy's haircut. I mean, it is just cut as short as can be. It is cut just like Karl Myers' hair. And that's what I looked like when I moved back to Boston.

And that was pretty much the last time I got a haircut. The first two years I was in Boston, maybe three years, I didn't shave or cut my hair. I did get a perm at one point, and I have pictures of this too. And they had a joke at the office. They had a cartoon up on the wall of some hippy guy with long hair and a beard talking to his supervisor, and his supervisor was saying, "What happened to that nice, clean cut man that we hired two years ago?"

So anyway, so now I have got hair

down to the middle of my back and a beard. Maybe I have shaved my beard by now. And I am also, since I have such little captioning work to do here, I am also court reporting. So I am tucking my ponytail down the back of my suit jacket and taking depositions in downtown San Diego. And I am working in a place called Media Captioning. And life was pretty good.

One of the unfortunate things that happened during this period of time was, I was hanging out at a couple of different bars, and I met a guy when I was golfing a lot at this time. I had started golfing a lot while I was in Boston, so I was going around golfing a lot, and I went on a golf tournament, to Tijuana, Mexico, and I was just plastered on tequila and some guy offered me some cocaine.

Now, I had done cocaine before, and I should probably do a whole chapter on the cocaine years, but I didn't like it and I hadn't done cocaine for several months at that point. And it really hurt my nose, but the guy taught me how to smoke it or freebase it, as we say in cocaine terms, and I started freebasing coke pretty regularly.

I wouldn't have considered myself a

freebase addict at that point. I was an alcoholic and I was a drunk, but I started smoking a lot of cocaine, and I was smoking and snorting and drinking a lot.

And my job never really took off too well. but I never really liked working for Media Captioning. I didn't really like the owners of the company and I wasn't making a heck of a lot of money there. Things weren't really going that good.

And then my parents made the mistake of helping me buy a house that I didn't really want that had an expensive mortgage on it that I couldn't afford, and they were convinced, because they hadn't seen me for several years, and because of the rumors that I was this great captioner who had accomplished all of these things and been on TV and because I had sold stock in a company and had a lot of money, at that particular time, that I would be able to afford this house. And I was just blowing it.

I mean, I went through my money quick, and within a short period of time, I wasn't able to afford the house payments nor the taxes, and it turned into a nightmare, and it is probably something I will talk about at some point on this tape, but suffice it to say that that house became a real burden to me, and eventually they fired me from the job too. And then I started trying to court report full time again and I hated

I am living in a house that I can't afford. I am not making very much money. I have been fired from my job at Media Captioning. I have gone to work for a court reporting company. And a nice lady, Cindy Mandigo, who I had trained in captioning at Media Captioning, is helping me get court reporting work.

She is also very interested in setting up her own captioning business and has introduced me to some people in Newport Beach called RapidText, and they sold captioning equipment and also were trying to start a business. And at one point, they wanted me to head up a real time project for the not asbestos litigation. I had been on asbestos litigation many, many years before. They wanted me to head up a project for the implants for I can't even remember the name of it. Silicone, for silicone.

And they gave me about a 200 page manual of all the terms that would come up. I had 50 attorneys. It was going to be an original and 50 copies. I was going to be in charge of about five different court reporters and scheduling and setting it all up. I was going to be the main court reporter on it. I would have made between $10,000 and $20,000 a week, I believe, with an original and 50 copies daily, and I was going to be doing about 50 pages a day at $50 a page, so you can figure it out.

It was going to be a huge project. And my alcoholism had just spiraled out of control, because I wasn't working and I wasn't paying my mortgage and my parents were just besides themselves, and they realized they made a huge mistake. They didn't know who I was. And my mother now wants me to go to treatment, and I am about 35 years old, 36, maybe.

And I said to her I will never forget. I said, I don't care how messed up I am right now or how much I am drinking right now. The day this silicone litigation starts, when I go up to Newport, I am going to clean up. I am going to get on my suit and tie. I am going to get into my hotel room and I am going to get down to business. And I know I have got good work ethic, and that's the way it is going to be.

She said, You better get clean before

then. You better start now. But this was going to be my manna from heaven, because I was far in debt. All of my credit cards were maxed. I had blown all the money that I had made from my stock sale. Nothing was left. I had very little money coming in.

Besides being a drunk and I had a cocaine habit, I was bouncing checks. I was writing checks on accounts that had been closed for years. I was suffering severe depression. It just seemed like my life was really coming to an end.

I was playing guitar. I was making a little bit of money giving guitar lessons and playing guitar at a couple of little coffeehouses, and I just I really was beside myself. But I was sure that this job was going to get me back in the black. This was going to pay off all my credit card bills. It was going to get me back on track with my home in Cardiff, and it was going to make me also a renowned court reporter doing this huge litigation for the silicone litigation. I mean, it was really going to be big.

And I had my new computerized software and I had my new laser printer and my new court reporting machine, and I was really gearing up. Even though I was drunk, I was really gearing up for this job. And what happened was, about two weeks before the job started, they settled and my services were no longer needed.

And you talk about getting thrown into a severe depression. I just gave up. I literally just gave up on life at that point. I said, What is the use? I am never going to get out of this.

I started selling some illegal substances just to get by. I would basically sit in a bar all day long. I would drink all day long, sip cocktails, drink beer, take shots of tequila, play pool, play darts, and sell small amounts of whatever, marijuana, cocaine to people at the bar, and then I would go home between midnight and 2:00 o'clock in the morning, and I would freebase cocaine until 6:00 o'clock in the morning, 5:00 or 6:00 o'clock in the morning, take some Valium, drink some more beers or cocktails, go to sleep, wake up and start all over.

And to tell you the truth, I can't remember how long this went on. I don't know if it was a year or two years, but basically from age 35 to 42, this was pretty much my MO. And at one point, Media Captioning gave me my job back, and I started trying to get sober.

I went to Alcoholics Anonymous when I was 35, right about the same time, and I was able to stay sober at one point for about a moth and a half, but I just couldn't hang in there, especially after this thing with the silicone trial going down the tubes. I just I became worse than I had ever been in my life.

I had been a horrible drunk in my twenties, and I will talk more about that later, but I have always been able to rise to the occasion when I needed to. I had a work ethic that always pulled me up when I needed to be pulled up and got to work and did my job and made my money and paid my bills, but now I am at a point from 36, maybe 36, 37, and I just got nothing left.

I am completely drained and I have no job, and I think probably I get the job back at Media Captioning and it works for a while. And finally one day, they call me in, and I had passed out drunk at work, and they didn't believe me. They thought I was kidding and they thought that, for some reason, that they knew that I had tried to start a captioning company before and they believed that this was my way of sabotaging their business, so I could steal their clients.

And they asked me for the key to the office and they fired me. And I was just in tears. I was about 38 or 39 years old, and I just didn't know what I was going to do. That had pretty much been my last hope, and I had been trying to get sober off and on, but I just gave up.

I ended up getting a job at a gas station here in Encinitas, and I was seeing a girl at this time too, and she was just as bad as I was, and she started having an affair with one of my roommates, and I got pissed off one day and tried to run him off the road. And I won't go into the whole story, but eventually, after I got him run off the road and got the girl back in my car, we got in an argument while we were driving back to my house, and I went off the side of the freeway and crashed that car.

And so now I have got no car, no job. I am living on handouts and making a little bit of money here and there. I have got the gas station job. I lose the gas station job too. I pawned all my guitars. I pawned everything that is worth anything. I have been arrested and I am fighting a court case. It just looks really bad. I think I was arrested twice that year.

And so anyway, I decide well, I am going to stop right here. I am at a point where I am about ready to kill myself. I am really suicidal, and I just don't know what to do. And my girlfriend tells me, she actually suggests that I commit suicide.

She says, You are such a lowlife piece of crap, you might as well just kill yourself. You have nothing to live for. You are worthless. And at that point, I was about 39 years old, I think, 39, maybe 40.

Okay. So here we are. I am suicidal. I am basically unemployable. I am living at a house that I used to own, that I have signed over to my parents, because I am no longer capable of making payments. I am supposed to be paying rent to them and taking care of the house and getting rent from other tenants that live there. I am not capable of doing that either.

I have had all of the utilities turned off and the phone turned off and spent all the money from the tenants, so now my parents are forced to drive 200 miles every month to either collect the rent and also have been forced to put all of the utilities under their name to keep the utilities turned on for the house.

The whole thing is a nightmare, even more for my parents, probably, than me. They are just so disappointed in what they thought. You know, they thought the homecoming of their son from Boston, who had been successful in this new captioning adventure and selling his stock and making a lot of money, and it is time to return and get a nice home to live in San Diego and get married and settle down and have kids and give them grandchildren.

And instead, my drinking continues to spiral out of control, and on top of that, I add cocaine to it. So I guess we can pretty much end this up. San Diego is just a total bust.

And so I call my parents one day and I tell them I am like about ready to end it, and they drive 120 miles an hour from Palmdale to San Diego, pick me up. I don't know why. For some reason, I didn't have any shoes. I had a pillowcase that I stuffed some clothes in. They went and bought me a pair of shoes and they gave me $20 and they drove me off to my old friend's house, Ken Olson, who was in the band.

Ken Olson and Steve Gates were still talking to me. Jeff Basenberg was still up in Box Canyon. So I am up in Los Angeles now. I am starting to do some painting work for my friends, and I am living on a couch, and I am not using cocaine, but I am drunk every day still.

But anyway. So eventually, after I do some odd jobs here and there for a few weeks, Ken Olson gives me a job at his factory, MMI Industries, and I become a first doing odd jobs, and then I become a machinist. And I am pretty good at it, and then eventually they start giving me office work too.

And I move into Steve Gate's house. I have a bedroom with a little TV and a single bed. I don't have too much of anything else. But it is a real beautiful house, so I am living pretty good. I have food, and I had been hungry for a long time. So I have all the food I can eat, all the booze I can drink, and a job. And it is a pretty hard job. I am working usually from 6:00 in the morning until 4:00, 5:00 o'clock in the afternoon.

I get 45 minutes for lunch, at which time I either go to a strip bar or a liquor store and pick up a quart of beer and go to the park and drink it. And one day, I have some problems after maybe I had two quarts, and I broke a machine at the machine shop that cost several thousand dollars. I didn't set it up right.

And so my good friend, Ken Olson, who also drinks heavily, but seems to keep his shit together, whereas I don't, tells me, No more drinking at lunchtime. And I am like, now now the world has come to an end. I can't even drink at lunchtime.

But anyway, I continue drinking at lunchtime. And I have been there about three or four months now, and he also takes me out to happy hour every day after work, and I get unlimited drinks on the company credit card, and I have food, and my rent is paid and I have a few extra dollars. So I am feeling like things are going pretty good.

And for some reason, I don't remember how it came about, out of the blue, this job offer came up to do closed captioning in Pittsburgh. Now, Ken tells me, Don't go. Things are going good for you here. You just stay.

And a few weird things had happened while I was up in L.A., and I am not going to talk about them at length on this tape, but I will say that I had a slight cocaine relapse that involved a girl, and it turned into a nightmare, and I was ready to get fired even from my best friend's machine shop.

Chapter 15

The Pittsburgh years

Last chance, death on the horizon, the most excruciating nightmare of my life, drunken, sex filled orgy of decadence.

So anyway, I went on an interview to Pittsburgh. I didn't even have enough money to pay for my room when I got there. I thought it was paid for. So I get there. I am sitting at the bar all night getting drunk, and I don't have any money to pay for my room, and eventually I don't remember how it happened. I get in the room, and I get to the job interview the next day. I am completely out of my mind. It is a two day job interview, where I have to do a whole series of about four or five hours of academic tests and then another whole series of captioning tests.

I passed the captioning tests with flying colors. I had a few problems with the academics. I hadn't really brushed up for many years. I am 40, 41 years old at this time. No. I am 40. I am 40 years old. It is October of 1995.

Anyway, they tell me I smell funny. In other words, you have got booze on you, but we are willing if you clean your act up and we will hire you and we will pay all of your moving expenses to come back here and give you a one year contract. We will give you a lot of money. I forgot what it was. Maybe $45,000 a year, plus medical benefits, and pay all of your moving expenses.

So I don't know how I am going to get back there. I don't have a car. I don't have any money. I tell my parents about it, and they are excited as all hell, and my dad makes the mistake of loaning me a credit card. In the meantime, I also somehow get his identification and his Social Security number and so forth.

They rent me a car. I drive cross country. I am sober. I haven't had a drink in two or three days, and I stop in Laughlin, Nevada on the way there. I am just going to have one drink. Anyway, I start drinking at Laughlin, Nevada. And I don't remember the sequence of events, but I drank my way across the country, across Route 66 to Pittsburgh.

And I was in a motel for a couple of

days there, and they wanted me to hurry up and start work. I said, Well, I have got to find a place to live. And I had to find the perfect place to live. So I did.

I found a place that was right next to a bus line that was on top of a bar. It was connected to a bar upstairs and had a laundromat across the street, and my I am now in Pittsburgh on Mount Washington. And my theory is, I won't get arrested for driving under the influence, because I am drinking right underneath my house, and I have a bus stop right in front, so I will take the bus right to work.

And there is also a gondola. It is a very strange situation. So I take a bus to work in the morning, and on the way home, I walk across a river that is a part of Three Rivers Stadium from Pittsburgh. First I stop at a bar on the way home on one side of the bridge. Then I get across the bridge and I take this gondola up a mountain, to Mount Washington. Then I stop at a bar at the top of Mount Washington and I walk about another mile to my apartment, which is on top of a bar, and then I drink at that bar all night.

Now, they changed my hours several times at Vitac, because first I think they had me on early mornings. And apparently, I was just out of my mind with a hangover every morning, when I came in early mornings. So they said, well, let's put you on late nights.

Now I am drinking in the bar every day until 3:00 or 4:00 in the afternoon and going in in the evening and working from 4:00 to midnight. Even my bartender is saying, Ed, you have got to quit drinking so much before work. You are going to get fired.

I pass out two nights in a row while I am captioning the Jay Leno Show, and I have now been there seven weeks. I have used up all of my sick days and all of my vacation time, and I haven't taken advantage of my medical benefits to do anything.

I need to be detoxed. I have a lot of teeth problems. My teeth are falling out of my head from abuse. I haven't had a checkup in years. I am broke, I am hungry, and I get fired. And my daily schedule, up to that point, had been go to work drunk, leave at dinner break, try to limit myself to two drinks, come home and drink all night. And I am living with a girl that I have met, who is very questionable. She has drug problems. I am an alcoholic. I also have drug problems.

We start to go to 12 step meetings. We are going to get clean and sober. We are going to move to San Diego together and get married and get clean and sober and have a wonderful life.

And her and her girlfriends are partying over at my place, and I get fired. And what happens is, shortly after I get fired, I win $1,000 on a football pool for the Super Bowl in 1996. I believe I can't remember for sure, but I think it was the Pittsburgh Steelers against the San Diego Chargers. Anyway, I win $1,000. Maybe it was more. And I go on quite a run.

And I have an eviction notice on my door. I have now, because of my great work ethic, taken a job working for minimum wage at a demolition company. And the job I am working on, it is in the middle of winter, it is in January, now January of '96. I am 41 years old and my job is helping tear down houses that have been burnt up and like dig up the concrete basements and pull shit out of the walls and carry it in wheelbarrows outside and dump it.

I mean, it was exhaustive work. I lost a lot of weight. I would get paid daily, and the way he would pay me is, he would meet me at the bar underneath my house, which I was getting evicted from, and he would pay me at the bar. And whatever I made that day I would drink that night.

I let my parents know about the situation. Actually, what I did was, I stole my father's identity with his credit card, because our names are very similar, and I burned them for, I think between $8,000 and $10,000. And I drank and used that money in a period of a month or two, and eventually they found out about it, and my mother sent me a bus ticket.

It is now Easter of 1996. I am just dead broke. I don't even have enough money to pay for a taxicab to get to the bus station, but I call a taxi anyway. I have been up all night drinking. I have got a bus that is leaving at probably 8:00 in the morning. I can't remember. A taxi gives me a ride to the bus station. I am late. He asked for his money. I have got about $2.50 and some food stamps. I start pulling the change out of my pocket, and he realizes that I am a deadbeat, and he takes my bags out of the trunk and throws them in the street. And the bus is starting to leave the station, and I am screaming for the bus to stop and running with my bags.

Oh. Besides that, I didn't get my last paycheck, because since I broke the contract with the company, not only did I not get my last paycheck, they claimed I owed them about $4,000 in moving expenses, so I had no it was just a nightmare.

And everything I owned was in Pittsburgh. I had had everything I owned shipped out there, because they paid for it. And I left my guitar and my bowling ball and my golf clubs, I think, with my bartender, and I shipped home as much as I could ship own. Maybe 20 or 30 packages I shipped back to somewhere. I can't even remember if I shipped them to my parents or to San Diego.

But I was on this three or four day bus ride. It was a total nightmare. Somebody, for some reason, gave me a carton of cigarettes. I had no money, no food, no cigarettes, nothing.

And I showed up at my parents on Easter Sunday, 1996, and it was I am not even going to tell you what was said. My father answered the door and all he could say was, Mother, your son is here.

And I was glad to sit down to a Thanksgiving dinner, because I hadn't had a good dinner in a long time.

So anyway, Pittsburgh was a bust. I have left everything behind. The girlfriend and her two girlfriends that were staying with me are all dead today. They have all died from drug overdoses or heart attacks or whatever. They are all dead. The bartender ended up becoming a Border agent out here in San Diego, and it's funny.

But anyway, so I am at my parents' house. They are trying to nurse me back to health. I am very sick. Oh. And while I was in Pittsburgh, the last week I was there, first, because of something I said I was involved or knew somebody that was in the Mafia, and one of his daughters wanted to come over to my house, and I said some really rude things to her. I don't know what. But anyway, two people were hired to beat the shit out of me, and they pulled up in a big pickup truck and as I was walking out of the bar they pummelled me to the ground and beat me to a pulp.

A couple of days after that, another kid who was in my apartment, for one reason or another, got in a fist fight with me and, fortunately, my girlfriend and her friends pulled him off of me. He beat me to shit. So I got bruised ribs, black eyes, a swollen head, and this is the condition that I showed up at my parents in.

So while I am at my parents, I am now in Palmdale, and I stayed there for about a month. And I should probably stop right now, but since I am on a roll, I will keep going. While I am there, I steal every bit of loose change I can find in their house. I steal as much booze as I can. I steal all their pills from their cabinet. But I am getting better, because I am actually working.

Once again, the work ethic kicks in. I am working about eight or nine hours a day, doing hard labor around their house, clearing weeds, planting, doing landscaping, doing whatever I can to help out around there. And I am eating. I am eating a lot. And I am sneaking away, now and then, with a few dollars in my pocket and getting a few beers or a couple of shots of liquor.

I am not getting a lot of booze, but I am getting enough to satisfy me, and I am claiming sobriety. So anyway, I pretty much, at this point, look hopeless. I am 41 years old. It is 1996. I tell my parents I am going to go back to San Diego and find a place to live and get a job as a dishwasher or busboy or whatever I can do.

And finally, they agree to drive me to San Diego and let me stay in the house that I had basically ruined while I was there before. And I am going to get sober. I am going to go back to meetings and I am going to get sober.

And what happened was, about a week after I got there, the company that had fired me twice already, Media Captioning I had called them from Pittsburgh and asked them if they could hire me back, and they said under no circumstances. But out of the blue, they showed up at my house and put a note on my door, We would like to interview you.

So I get my job back at Media Captioning, and I am kind of half ass sober, but not really. So I would say this is April, May, June, July, August. In August, I am in a really bad way. They are ready to fire me again at Media Captioning. I am holed up at a hotel drunk out of my mind, and I say, Okay, I am done.

And August 2nd, 1996, I get sober,

and I think it is for good. And they let me keep my job, and I don't take a drink for 119 days, 119 days.

Chapter 16

Coming Back to San Diego, 1996

And so now I am back in San Diego. I have gotten my job back at Media Captioning again and almost lost it again. It is August 2nd, 1996, and I am getting sober. And I am sure that this is the last time, and I am going to stay sober for the rest of my life. Okay? And I will continue back on this in a little while.

So here I am, clean and sober, and I think I really got this thing down. I guess I just better fast forward. Anyway, the job goes really good for a few months. I save some money. I am making new sober friends. I am really committed to staying sober, and I am paying back my debts.

I have a lot of high hopes. And I can't really say exactly what happened, except that one night I decided I wanted to have a beer. And then I decided I wanted to have a six pack. And then I decided I should have a cocktail. And that cocktail lasted for four and a half months.

That would have been the day after Thanksgiving, 1996. So November 29th, 1996, I took a drink and that drink took me on a ride, and that drink just completely humiliated me again. I got to a point where I couldn't go to work. They didn't know what was the matter with me. I went to a doctor, I believe, around the beginning of April.

He tried to help me detox on Valium. I wasn't going to work. I was sending my work, Media Captioning, I was sending them reports from my doctor that I was disabled, and they wanted to meet with me. And I just couldn't meet with them. I was just too out of it. I couldn't get any hours together sober enough to meet with them. And I really didn't know what I was going to do.

I just figured, you know, everything was over. I will say that within like a few weeks after that drink on Thanksgiving night, my work had put me on probation, and I was just barely hanging on. I was just barely hanging on there for months. I knew it was the end again.

I went in to see a doctor on October

8th or 9th, and I hit a car in the parking lot. So I was going to get sober that day. I went in and I filled out all of the paperwork, and I went into a hospital or detox facility. And they said, Okay. Let's show you to your room. And I am like, Right now? I left my door unlocked at my house. I have got to go lock my house up.

They probably looked at me like this guy is out of his mind. Anyway, I went home. A little while later, a cop shows up at my door. Somebody said they saw your car hit a car in this parking lot.

Anyway, somehow I was able to talk that cop out of taking me to jail. I promised I would pay the person off and everything. And I drank for the rest of that day and the rest of that night. And I made a commitment that night while I was laying in bed. I said, I am going to try this one more time. This is it, one more time, and I am going to just be absolutely thorough. I am going to do everything it takes to stay sober this time.

And not only did I go into a detox facility the next day, I moved into a sober living facility with about 50 other guys. It was pretty humiliating. I had nothing. I lost everything once again. And basically, what I had when I moved into that place was, my sister gave me a sleeping bag and a lamp, and somebody in the sober living place gave me a TV, which I put on a cardboard box. It was a little 13 inch black and white TV.

And so that is how I started my journey into sobriety, and that was April 10th, 1997. As I am speaking right now, it is August 16th, 2012, so that has been 15 years, four months and two days. And I will say I am going to talk a lot about my journey in sobriety, but one thing I will say hasn't happened in 15 years is I haven't been arrested again. I haven't been in a fight again. I haven't been drunk again. I haven't stolen anything. I have made new friends. I have reconnected with my mother and my sister. And it was really hard with my sister, because I had hurt my family so much.

I was able to become friends with my father before he passed away. I was a couple of years sober then. And so a lot of great things happened. I went to work doing menial jobs. First, I did a little landscaping and did a little ditch digging. I did a little I used to clean a restaurant called Johnny Rockets at 3:00 or 4:00

o'clock in the morning. I would go in there and clean with another guy who had a contract with them.

And then after a few months, I got a job working at a pottery shop for $40 a day with Joey Correo. Correo's Pottery. And after a few months, I got a raise to $50 a day. I worked there five or six days a week. So I am making a little money. It is an easy job. I just sit around and basically read 12 step literature and have sober friends come in and visit with me.

So that was a good time in my life. I was starting to feel comfortable being sober finally, because I hated sobriety. I have a few stories about that too. But at first, it was just horrible being sober, but I had really made a commitment that this was it. I am really, really going to try and do this again.

I just don't see that I have another chance. I go out one more time, I am going to be living on the street. That's it. I have lost all my friends. I have lost all my family. I have lost everything that means anything to me. I am never going to be a court reporter or closed captioner again.

That part of my life is over, as far as I

am concerned. But after about nine months of working at the pottery shop, a girl named Cindy Mandigo, who I had trained in captioning in 1988, I believe, '88 or '89, at Media Captioning, offered me a little job working one hour a day, working as a captioner.

And I told her I couldn't do it. I told her I hocked all of my equipment. I didn't have any machines or computers or anything, and I really didn't think I had the mental capacity to do that kind of work anymore.

And she kept pestering me about it. She pestered me about it for months. And finally one day, I said, How much would this pay? And she told me, and it would have been twice as much for that hour as I was making per day.

So I said, Well, I will give it a shot, but what do I do for equipment? And they helped me out. She helped me out with it, with a company up in Newport called RapidText. I went up there, and I still knew a theory and so forth. And he was working on a beta program. It was a new captioning program. They weren't selling it, and it was in DOS. A lot of people were already on Windows. I had already worked with him on my dictionary and on some rules for the captioning program.

And they give me a computer and a stenotype machine and a program to test at home, and they give it to me for a total of I don't know if it was I think it was $100 or $150 a month that I would pay them, and I started captioning a show called I started practicing on CNBC, and eventually I ended up captioning one hour a day from 5:00 to 6:00, a show called Geraldo, and I am sure many people have heard of Geraldo. And I was making $500 a week for doing that one hour a day, and I was still working at the pottery shop making $250 a week, for a 40 hour week.

But I stayed busy and I stayed very involved in 12 step fellowship and very involved in working with other people and trying to help other alcoholics and drug addicts. I used to go to a detox, into a hospital and speak a lot and I went to a lot of meetings, so I guess I am breaking my anonymity in this book, but I am well, I guess I don't have to say I am a member of anything. I will just say I was involved in a program where I was committed to sobriety and to try to help other people stay sober.

So anyway, that is where my

captioning career began again, and that would have been probably I started actually working, I practiced for about two months and I started working in about March, April of 1998, and I was probably about one year sober at that time.

And I will go on a little bit from here and get into it. I don't know. Three or four months later, I met a girl that I fell in love with and we got engaged, and that didn't work out. And something always happens around Thanksgiving or Christmas, I guess.

Thanksgiving of 1998, I guess it would have been, she decided she wasn't going to go out with me anymore. Not only was she not going to go out with me anymore, she was going to go out with another guy that I knew that was barely sober and move into his van.

And I thought I was doing so good, and I was sober for over a year and a half, and I had a place to live and a career on the upswing, and I got left for a loser, which made me feel like even more of a loser. And I will say that I wanted to drink every single day, every single waking minute of my life from that period for about, probably over three months.

About two months after that, I lost the

contract with Geraldo Rivera, and it really looked like things weren't working out too well. I had saved a little bit of money and I had a couple thousand dollars, and I was talked into investing it into a new computer and writing up a resume and contacting some other captioning agencies, which I was scared to do because of my past.

I had been fired from almost every captioning agency in the United States. Everybody knew who I was, because I was one of the founders of real time closed captioning and I had worked for or with almost every captioning company in the United States at that time, and if I hadn't worked for them, they had heard of me and they had heard that I was bad news.

So anyway, I put out this resume, and I was going broke and I was ready to drink and I was miserable, and it was now January of 1999. And right about that same time, Bill Clinton was involved in an impeachment hearing, and that was a blessing for me, because I got hired to caption several hours a day of that hearing, and all of a sudden I was making more money in the next couple, two or three months than I had made in the last year.

So things just progressed from there.

And now here I am several years later, the business was very, very profitable for me, and I became a workaholic for a while. I am going stop here right now at the impeachment hearings of 1999, because I have got to do something when the impeachment is over, and we will and I am going to quit saying "and" also.

The captioning business became very profitable. I became very involved in working for several different companies. I apologized to a lot of the companies that I had had bad experiences with, and they began to trust me and give me work.

I worked from my house and I worked with that beta program, and I am saying "and" again. Anyway, I better I will just wrap that part up for right now. And it just captioning became a very important part of my life, along with staying sober.

I loved working and I also loved making money for a change and improving my life. So that was a big deal for the next couple of years. I stayed very involved in a sobriety program and I stayed very involved in working and trying to organize a business and a file and becoming a member of society again.

It was hard for me to get electricity and a phone and a cellphone. I had to leave $1,000 deposits with people, because I had wrecked my credit with everybody, and it was a chore for me just to get a cable TV set up. So these were a lot of the things I had to go through in my first few years of sobriety, trying to reestablish a life.

I guess, at about the summer of 1999, when everything is going good and I have now been captioning for about six months and it looks like there might be a life ahead.

How did I live one more time to get his 189th chance at life? Back to San Diego, 1996.

Anyway, let's get back to 1999, the summer of 1999. I have gotten sober. I have returned from Pittsburgh. It was just a mess, that whole experience from, I guess it would have been October 1995 until Easter of 1996. It was just the most excruciating nightmare of my life.

Anyway, summer of 1999, things are going good. Captioning business is picking up. The house that I signed back over to my parents is finally going to be sold. My father is dying, and we have gotten to be friends, which has been good.

And so anyway, he passed in the fall of '99. And Keith Booth, who was a good friend of mine, who I will talk about more, went to the funeral with me. I spoke at that funeral, and Keith and I went to Vegas directly afterwards, with no suitcases or planning. That was an interesting trip.

I worked really hard. I mean, I am trying to remember a lot. I can't remember a lot about 1999, but I had moved into a really nice house in Carlsbad on Lavender Way. It was a private community. It was beautiful. It had a lake and pathways and very quiet, a nice three bedroom house. I turned one of the rooms into an office overlooking the ocean. I started a meeting at the house, a 12 step meeting called The Sunday Seekers, where we read from the big book.

What is funny is, I had been to some 12 step meetings in my well, once in my teens and a couple of times in my twenties, and I am just kind of reverting here a little bit. But I just thought they were so ridiculous, and they are kind of hokey. But I just thought it was so stupid, the whole big book and all of the rules and everything, and especially the no drinking, not even beer.

But in my early 30s, when I was in Boston, I was taking somebody to AA meetings. It was court ordered. His name was Blue. And one day, I went to pick him up and he wasn't there. So I went to the bar and I said, "Hey, what happened to Blue? I was going to take him to his meeting and he is not there."

And they said, "Blue killed himself." And I said to myself, you see what that AA does? It makes people feel guilty about drinking and then they go out and kill themselves. So I didn't go to another meeting for about five years after that.

But anyway, so now I am all wrapped up in AA. I am all about God and I am all about staying sober and helping others and having this meeting at my house, and I am just on fire about sobriety and the big book that I used to think was so hokey. So it is a pretty good life. I am pretty happy at this time.

A few things happen. Actually, an old friend of mine, who had tried to help me get sober years ago, I ran into him in a detox facility. He had relapsed, and so I was helping him, and I let him move into my house over there too.

Chapter 17

Australia 2000 Olympics

I got a call from some people who were working, putting together some captioners to close caption the 2000 Olympics in Australia.

And they didn't have very many people over there with a lot of captioning knowledge at that time. They were on a completely different system, in fact, than I was. So they asked me if I would be interested in going over there. And I thought to myself, well, I am on like three years sober. I can't leave my home. I can't go to Australia.

And they had offered me $1,000 a day, plus all of my expenses. And so anyway, I talked to somebody about it, and he said, hey, they have Alcoholics Anonymous in Australia. You can go to Australia.

Anyway, I told them I would accept the job. It was quite a challenge. I had to send them my closed captioning dictionary, which is something that I am not going to try to get into the whole explanation of in this novel, but I have a dictionary that is prepared for my particular captioning software here in America, and it doesn't match up with the software in Australia.

So I send them my closed captioning dictionary, which contains every word in the English dictionary, plus all of the names and countries and all of the athletes that are going to be in the Olympics and everything, and they convert it for me over there, and get it all ready for me to use on their software.

I show up in Australia. I am met by a member of Alcoholics Anonymous at the airport, and I get very involved in Alcoholics Anonymous over there and immediately start sponsoring somebody.

I don't know if I should talk about this in a book or not or how to work around the language. I am supposed to be staying anonymous, I believe. But anyway, I went to a 12 step program. Let's just say I went to a 12 step program over in Australia and got very involved and had a lot of fun, went to a lot of pot lucks and parties, and at the same time I was involved working for Channel 7, Australia.

At this time, I was in Perth. Even though the Olympics were in Sydney, I was working at a television station in Perth. And it was wonderful. Within a few days, I had the software all figured out and they were praising me. Kangaroos were running wild on this TV station, parrots and beautiful birds, and I just loved the city of Perth.

I just had such a wonderful time there, and I met good friends and I traveled up and down the west coast on my free time, west coast of Australia, and I knew that one day I would go back there.

I had a blast closed captioning the Olympics. I made a lot of money. I felt proud. I was interviewed by a very prominent magazine over there that was involved with the Olympics and with closed captioning or something. And I have a copy of the magazine somewhere, but they did a whole interview with me. And it was exciting, you know, to be an important part of history, of the 2000 Olympics in Sydney.

I also started buying gold at that time and getting involved in saving coins again. I had sold all of my coins or pawned them or traded them for drugs earlier in life, and so now I started buying gold. It was only $250 an ounce at that time. I went to the Perth mint and I bought Olympic coins and I bought gold coins and I bought gold nuggets.

I just had an absolute blast there. And while I was there, my taxi driver said, If you like traveling around the world, I think you would like Thailand. So I got home from the Olympics, and I don't know, I guess it would be in November over in Australia, it is summer in November.

Chapter 18

Thailand Grabs my Heart, Australia, Thailand, San Diego, Back and forth.

So anyway, I got home from the Olympics and I bought a plane ticket to go to Phuket, Thailand in 2000, and I went over to Phuket, Thailand for ten days.

And the first two girls, I met I fell in love with one at a time, but the second one, I was going to get a fiance visa for her and bring her to America. On my way home, I met a beautiful girl, Thai girl on the airplane. We were stuck in Korea together for eleven hours on a layover. She spoke no English and I spoke no Thai. I have videotapes of this excursion. I have a lot of photos. Now I am taking a lot of photos. I have become a real photo bug, now that I am clean and sober.

And she was a beautiful girl. Her name was Bee, and I never thought I would have a chance with her. She came from a very wealthy family. And she had a talking dictionary, a little computer, so she would speak Thai and I would speak English and we would figure out what each other was saying. And I figured out she was going to an English language school in Los Angeles, and eventually, she was going to go to college, either Riverside UC College or San Francisco or something.

She gave me a call a week or so later and said she hated the school she was in in Los Angeles and wanted to visit me in San Diego. She was extremely shy. She slept on my couch for about a week. I was 46, just turned 46. She was young. She was 21 or 22, and I don't know. I was just beside myself. I loved the whole thing. And eventually she wanted to marry me. She had to go to San Francisco to visit some wealthy relatives, and then her parents decided she was going to go to college in Seattle, Washington, and I decided I would move up there.

She called me one day and she said, "I hate it in Seattle. I want to move down to San Diego. And if you will marry me, I will sign a prenup." And I said, okay. And the next day, she called me up crying, and she said my parents have told me if I get married before I get my master's degree that I will no longer be their daughter. And that, I believe, might have been the last time we talked. We became out of contact, and I think eventually she realized that 21 year old girls in the United States usually go out with guys in their twenties, and she lost interest in me, and we broke up.

And since that time, now, many, many years later, eleven years later, I have made 40 or 50 round trips to Thailand. I own property over there. Also, learning to speak the Thai language and renovating properties.

I would say the summer of 2000. I have now gone back to Thailand twice already, and I am trying to get a business started over there. I have saved some money and I am working harder than ever. I have decided if I want to live in Thailand or start a business, I need to make some serious money.

And up to this point, I was making money, but I would go to Mexico once a month, Palm Springs once a month, I would go to Vegas every few months, and I had fun. I was spending my money as I made it. I had finally got myself a decent little car for a few thousand dollars. I was almost out of debt. I was paying off the IRS still.

Eventually, after being sober for six years, I ended up paying off I wouldn't say I paid off $80,000 in debt, but I came to a settlement altogether, and I don't know how much money I gave eventually. I gave my parents a lot of money. I gave the IRS a lot of money. I paid back all of the bad checks that I wrote. I paid back all of the liquor stores and the bars.

And we call it, in 12 step terminology, we call that making amends. I made financial amends to everyone I owed money to. And I continue to, any time that I wrong somebody today, to make amends as quickly as possible and admit my wrongs.

Anyway, so now I am working my ass off, and I am saving every penny that I am making. I am working, at this point, probably 50 hours a week, and it is now 2000, 2001. I am saving every penny that I make, and I am going to Thailand for about two to three weeks every three or four months.

And within about, I don't know I think in 2003, I had saved up quite a bit of money, and I wanted to move to Thailand, but I still didn't think I had quite enough. I was offered a job in Australia, full time in Sydney, Australia captioning.

So I left my beautiful home in Carlsbad. I shipped everything that I owned to Sydney, Australia. I got an apartment. I leased an apartment. I bought a car. I bought all brand new furniture. I found myself a Thai girlfriend, actually, she was my own age, over in Australia. Her name was Adie. I am Eddie and she is Adie. And it was wonderful. It really was.

I lived in Artarmon... I lived right near Bondi Beach. I will have to look at a map. It was near Crows Nest. It was right outside of the city of Sydney. My office was in Sydney and the TV station I worked at was about a two mile walk from my home, so I used to walk.

And for a long time, I took subways

or buses, and I walked everywhere, because I didn't like driving on the wrong side of the road. And I wish I would have kept walking. I lost a lot of weight doing that, and the car ended up being a waste of money.

I got ripped off on the car that I bought and ended up to make a long story short, it had been stolen and crashed and wrecked before I bought it and it was never fixed right and the title wasn't proper, and I ended up giving it to my girlfriend before I left Australia.

Part of the reason I went to Australia too is I was given a deal there that I could work every other month, so I would be closer to Thailand. Now I worked one month in Australia and lived one month in Thailand. So I am going back and forth from Australia to Thailand, and I am starting to look at more investment opportunities over there.

I might have bought my first condo in a building called Thien Thong in Jomtien on Soi 7 and Beach Road. It had a beautiful ocean view. So I bought that condominium, and I am going back and forth from Thailand to Australia.

And I am a chain smoker at the time also. And the reason I mention that is because I was working in a TV station, and for the five years prior to that, I had worked out of my house. I can't smoke in this TV station, so I have got to run outside every 30 minutes to light a cigarette. And also, I am working with a lot of people. I am working in a room with 40 or 50 TV monitors, a big TV station. There are people all around, and I have to look good. I don't know if I ever looked good, but I had grown my hair out for many years prior to this, so I have had long hair ever since 1985, ever since I went to Boston.

Within, I don't know, a period of months, I quit that job, and they were very unhappy with me because I had signed a one year contract and shipped everything I owned over there. I sold all the brand new furniture I had bought for that apartment in Australia at half price. I lost money on the leased apartment, condo that I had gotten. I gave my $4,000 car to my girlfriend, told her to sell it for whatever she could get and buy an airplane ticket to come to America with.

First she went to Thailand with me, and she did sell the car, I think, for 1,000 bucks and bought a ticket and came to Carlsbad. I had, by this time, leased a new condominium, a beautiful ocean view condominium on Paseo Del Norte. And it was a beautiful ocean view condominium, two story, two bedroom, two bath, two master bedrooms, a beautiful, big kitchen and patio.

She came out to stay with me, and we were thinking about getting married. Anyway, within about a month I don't know. We went on quite a few trips together. We went to Palm Springs together. We went to Vegas together. We enjoyed life together every day. And she thought I was working too much.

I am trying to save money. I am trying to put a life together. I am now, oh, 50 years old. No. I am older than that now. I am 53 years old and I am thinking, what am I going to do with my I mean, I have to get my life together. I have wasted the first 42 years and I am trying to save some money for retirement.

Anyway, we start to argue and she gives me an ultimatum: We get married by Christmas. So it would have been Christmas of 2004, I think. We get married by Christmas or I am going back to Australia. Needless to say, she went back to Australia.

We stayed in touch over the years. In

fact, in 2010, I went back to stay with her, ended up getting in an argument with her about three days after I got there, and that is another whole trip that I will talk about, but I stayed on the Gold Coast for about two weeks and learned how to surf during that period of time. And I have no regret for the relationship I had with that woman. She was a really, really nice lady, and that was a good time.

So 2004, I now have started working seven days a week, ten to twelve hours a day. I am saving money hand over fist, and everybody thinks I am out of my mind. I make it to meetings when I can, still very regularly, but like on break. You know, I will have like an hour break or 90 minute break and I will run to a 12 step meeting.

And I am still sober. I have been sober since April 10th, 1997, and we are now at 2004, 2005. I know a lot of years have gone by that I didn't talk about. Maybe I will think of something that happened during that period of time, but I think basically what happened during that period of time was I worked my ass off.

one of the things that happened during that period of time, in 2003, just before 2004, is I met a man named Karl Myers online, and it was a direct result of an article that I had written for a Thai web site called stickman.com, and I had written an article about Thailand and I owned a condo over in Thailand.

He had a Thai girlfriend in Texas, and he was a court reporter. And he noticed that my e mail name was eddiesteno, which stood for stenograph. So he wrote me an e mail and said, "Are you a court reporter?"

I said, "I used to be a court reporter, but now I do real time closed captioning."

He said, "Oh, I want to learn how to do that."

I said, "It is pretty difficult. I don't know if you want to really get into it. You know, you are going to have to buy like $6,000, $7,000 worth of software and do some training, even though you are already a court reporter."

And he called me or wrote me an e mail a few days later, and he said, "I bought the captioning software. What do I do now?"

At the time, I had a contract with CNBC captioning three or four hours a day. So I wrote him, I said, "You caption an hour a day of this program and you send me your file, and I will grade it and I will tell you how you are doing."

And I believe this was about November of 2003. I am pretty sure it was 2003, end of 2003, November. Yeah. Pretty sure. Anyway, yeah, it was, because I quit smoking in 2004, and when I met him, I was a smoker.

So anyway, what happened was, he was very diligent and he worked very hard, and within, I don't know, a month or less he was looking like he was almost ready to go on air.

At the time, I had about six girls helping me out taking different hours of captioning to fill in for me and also cover it all when I am going to Thailand for about three weeks every few months. You know, I have got a condo over there and I am trying to still set up a business. I am going to Thai school and learning the Thai language. I speak pretty good Thai now.

So I meet Karl, and the reason I have six girls working for me is, number one, the captioning industry is almost all women. And no offense, but a lot of them are very fickle with the hours they can work. And I have this three hours a day, seven days a week that I need to cover for CNBC.

And one girl will say, "I can do

Monday and Wednesday." And another girl will say, "I can do the first two hours on Thursday and the last two hours on Sunday." Another girl will say, "I can't work Friday night, but maybe I can do one hour on Saturday."

So I have got six girls to cover these seven nights a week, 21 hours of captioning. Twenty one hours of captioning is, I don't know, a pretty good chunk of money. It is thousands of dollars a month. Figure it out. Ninety hours of captioning a month, it's good work.

And I have got six girls doing it, and that is six girls to write paychecks to and six girls' personalities to deal with. And I am running back and forth to Thailand and trying to keep all of this put together, so when I come home I have my at least I have my CNBC contract and then any other freelance work I can pick up.

Anyway, I am in Thailand, and I am getting hassled by one or two or more of the employees. They want their money before I get home from Thailand. One of them decides she can't work certain hours. And I tell Karl about what is going on, and he says, "I will do it for you."

And I go, "What do you mean you will do it for me?"

He goes, "I will do all the hours."

I go, "But you have a full time job. You work in federal court."

He said, "Yeah, but in Texas, the hours are different." It was 5:00 to 8:00 in California. it would be 7:00 to 10:00 at night for him. So he goes, "I will do all of it."

And I was a little reticent about the whole thing until he said, "You don't even have to pay me for the first week or two." Something to that effect. I thought, this is a great deal.

And so my relationship was solidified with Karl, and he became the man who did all of my CNBC for me when I was in Thailand, some even when I was in the United States. A lot of times, I had worked starting at 4:00 o'clock in the morning. I worked for KUSI and San Diego from 5:00 in the morning until 9:00 or 10:00 o'clock every morning. I would take a nap, work for a few more hours, and then I would be on CNBC from 5:00 to 8:00 o'clock at night.

And usually by 6:00 or 7:00, I would be burnt, and I would send an instant message to

Karl and say, "Are you ready to take over on CNBC?" And, yes, he would. He was the most dependable person I ever met in my life, besides myself. So that was what happened.

And every time I went to Thailand, he did all of my work for me, and it was a great relationship, because he kicked me back a little percentage, ten percent or something of what we were making, so I could make a little money while I was in Thailand, and he made a great extra salary while I was gone too, and it allowed me a lot of ease of mind when I traveled.

The only problem was, to this point, I had never met Karl. We had only talked on the phone and through instant messaging and e mail. Maybe we had exchanged some photos. Also, when he would go to Thailand, because he traveled to Thailand on a regular basis, once or twice a year, I would let him stay in my condo over there.

Now, we never met, because when I was gone, he covered my work for me, and when he was gone, I had to make sure I stayed home to do the work. So that was the way that went for many years, I think at least four years. And one day, the contract with CNBC went away. No fault of our own. Just a contract change between rival captioning firms. And as a direct result of that, I was able to start seeing Karl. We could both go to Thailand at the same time.

We remain friends, and I gave him recommendations to other companies that I did closed captioning work, to make sure that he stayed employed and was able do some part time work, closed captioning. And we have become really, really close friends over the years, and it just has been a great relationship. Karl is an important part of my life, and he is even helping me with this dictation and whatever this turns into.

So I am now in 2005, 2006. All I can say about this whole time period from about 2005 to 2007 is, my health was in danger. I was working 70, 80 hours a week and taking off a few weeks every three or four months and going to Thailand.

And I think in about, I can't remember, Valentine's Day 2004, I quit smoking. I had about a two pack a day habit, so I am saving $3,000 a year now not smoking. Jesus Christ. In Las Vegas, cigarettes are $10 a pack now, as we speak in 2012. I am in San Diego, but they are still at least five bucks a pack here.

Anyway, I quit smoking. And my friend Mike Davidson helped me, and I want to talk a lot about Mike Davidson too. Mike Davidson is my closest friend in the world, and I trust him as much as anybody I have ever known in my life. He is just a really great, honest person, and he has helped me so much with staying clean and sober, and he was 100 percent responsible for making sure I stayed clean from cigarettes too, and I will be forever grateful to him for that.

About 2005, I decided I wanted to save some money, maybe 2006, I decided yeah, about 2006, I am going to save money. I am going to move out of this expensive two story condominium I have, where I live alone, and I am going to move into a little house, a little two bedroom, one bath house. I have a room about ten by ten that just barely fits my bed, with my friend Keith Booth, who we had a love hate relationship for years, but I have known him now since 1996. He knew me when I was trying to get sober and after I got sober, and we became real good friends, going to 12 step programs together and traveling to Las Vegas and Mexico together and going to a lot of meetings together.

And we had a love hate relationship, but we did love each other, and I moved in with him. And this house was great. I mean, it was 100 feet from the water. You could hear the waves breaking out the window. And it had a little, tiny bedroom there, and I set up my office in his living room. And I couldn't always work in the living room because Keith was very popular and he had a lot of friends over all the time.

So I had about a two foot walkway. Literally, I didn't have more than two fcct between my bed and the wall, and I set up an extra workstation in the bedroom. I had a satellite dish on the roof to help me with Canadian captioning.

And I worked my ass off while I lived there too. I kept working really hard. But the great thing there was, I now didn't have any contracts with anybody. I was only freelance. I only did work that was offered to me on a piecemeal basis, one week at a time schedule. So

I would take off for a month or two at a time, and I only had to pay $600 or $700 a month rent, and had Keith there to watch after my equipment and my mail.

So I would leave for months at a time and then go to Thailand and do what I do there, Basically, I went fishing and tried to fall in love and meet girls and got very involved in the 12 step programs over there, and also learned to speak Thai. I also started renovating condominiums over there. I had a period of time, over three or four years, where I renovated between 12 and 15 condominiums, and I still own three of those condominiums.

I am losing track of years now. It seems like when I get sober, I forget what years they are. I am not playing music as much anymore. I am living at Keith's. We are having a lot of fun. And so I guess that brings us up to about 2006. I wouldn't really know without looking at some bills or something, I am not sure, but I am going to guess it is about 2006 at that time.

And eventually, I get sick of living with him, and I say, "I have to move out." And I move back into a beautiful, another two bedroom condo overlooking the ocean that is 16 something a month, and I start busting my ass there and working harder than ever again. I think that was what I did.

And I got tired of that too. And about 2007, I am losing track of the years. Maybe I was at Keith's before 2006. By 2007, I moved in with Mike Davidson, a little two bedroom apartment. Once again, a little ten by ten foot room. I didn't even have a bed. My bed wouldn't fit in there. I just had a couch, my computer set up, and had a little storage space that I shared with Mike also. I didn't even have a parking spot for my car. We parked on the curb, but I was only two blocks from the beach and I loved it.

So I am living on Moonlight Beach. I am now, oh, traveling to Thailand for two to three months at a time and coming home and working for about six weeks at a time. I have saved a considerable amount of money. I have invested in a lot of condominiums and stocks, and I am doing pretty well. So that is what is happening. I am going to guess that those years are about 2007, 2008. And we had a very, very great relationship. I am such good friends with Mike. I really love him.

Mike decided that he was going to have his girlfriend move in with him, and also, he was going to move across the street into a great, big condominium overlooking the ocean. And there are some funny stories there too. He talked me into starting a web site called peacemanreview.com. And I can't put videos in the book, but I can put some photos on there.

What he started doing was, I like going to the movies, so I would go up on the roof of his condominium overlooking the ocean and he would videotape me. I would make 90 second clips of every movie I went to see and review it. The little catch was, I would do it with music, so I would play a little song: Peaceman got the movie review. It is a movie review for you. Might be good and it might be bad, might make you happy, might make you sad. And then I would go into a little 30 second spiel on the movie, play a little more music and leave it, and we posted all of these movies on my website and on Youtube.

We did about 50 or 55 of them. His girlfriend got kind of weird and he wasn't allowed to have friends coming over to his condo anymore. We better not put that in the book.

Anyway, for one reason or another, we quit doing the movie reviews. I still blog them to this day. I have been doing that for two or three years. And I moved into an apartment up on Encinitas, about a mile from Moonlight Beach, and I have been living here for about three or four years. It is a nice, little one bedroom apartment, $1,300 a month, which is too much. But I work for about three months at a time and then I go to Thailand for a month or two, and that is kind of where we are.

And I am still sober, by the way. It is 2012, August, and I have been sober for 15 years, four months and six days as I dictate this.

Okay. So when I come back to the dictation, we are going to do Thailand. Sex, sobriety, go go bars, girls, massage parlors and sobriety. Well, I don't know. We will come up with what is the title of this going to be? Thailand, land of smiles and much more. Go go bars, girls and sobriety in Thailand. Bye bye.

chapter 19

romance, go go bars, travel and frustration.

Okay. So I go to Thailand at the I guess it would actually I bought the ticket at the end of 2000 and ended up over there at the beginning of 2001. Immediately, I fall in love. I fall in love with a lady. I fall in love with the country. I want to learn the language. I love the food.

Much of Thailand is very, very beautiful, and then after the affects of love and being able to enjoy a country with wonderful food and for relatively modest prices, I start to see what is around me. And what I see around me is an undeveloped country. A lot of times, I run into infrastructure that I don't like. The streets aren't properly maintained.

There is a lot of corruption. There are a lot of strange smells in the air. Sometimes you might say the smells of untreated human waste. So it depends where you are. There are some very beautiful, nice, clean areas of Thailand and there are some very filthy, dirty areas. So I will talk a little bit about my travels in Thailand.

I started in Phuket and I stayed at a wonderful hotel right on the beach. Immediately, I met a wonderful girl and she stayed with me. One of the strange things about Thailand is, you fall in love and then you notice all around you, there are more women, especially if you are a man. You have go go bars everywhere. I never had been to a go go bar in my life.

You can go into a go go bar and there could be anywhere from half a dozen to four dozen topless women dancing on stage. And it is a little euphoric if you are not used to it. It is not like going into a strip bar in the United States, which I haven't done too often either, where one girl comes out on stage and dances. This is just like total flesh overload.

And then you have Thai massages everywhere, which are very inexpensive, depending on the exchange rate, anywhere from $3 to $10 for a nice one hour massage, and that is very nice also. The food, if you like Thai food, you can find meals everywhere from $1 to $100. There is such a wide range of food and places to go there.

But anyway, we were talking about travel, and I ended up, I started in Phuket, and I traveled all around Phuket and the islands and saw things that I had never seen before, ate food that I had never eaten before. I went to Bangkok and the Muay Thai boxing, went to the Floating Market, which I found just absolutely incredible.

And this is where the food pricing comes in too. That day I remember, I was with a lady, and we had some soup that was just incredible. It was a meal in itself, and I believe it was 50 cents a bowl for us. And that night my taxicab driver took me to one of the fanciest seafood restaurants in Bangkok, where I ordered I think a three or four kilo lobster and all of the trimmings and fresh vegetables and everything, and that meal came to over $150. So I ate for 50 cents in the afternoon and then $150 in the evening. Very unusual.

Now, also, when you are traveling, taxis are very inexpensive. Like a 100 mile taxi drive from the airport to Phuket or from Bangkok to Pattaya might be $50. In Phuket, there is a lot of double pricing, and you have to be careful what type of transportation you are taking. In Phuket, there are little, red buses that run around down there, and I wouldn't say it is expensive, but they do try to gouge the tourists.

Okay. So we are traveling. So I go to Phuket, to start with, and I go to Bangkok, and also travel to the islands, Phi Phi Island off of Phuket, James Bond Island. I go to a place called The Beach, which is where Leonardo DiCaprio filmed the movie The Beach.

And it was very exotic, very, very exotic, very nice, and I did meet a lot of nice people, and I became very interested in the country. Within three or four weeks, I flew back there and I had second thoughts of the whole thing. The girl that I had fallen in love with turned out to be a little more crazy than I had thought, and I didn't stay very long and I came back to America.

I can't remember the exact turn of events, but I had started cooking Thai at home and studying Thai, and then I had lived with the Thai girl I met on the airplane, and she had stayed with me, and I had made a decision that I did want to try to make an investment in Thai.

So I am studying Thai every day. I go back to Thailand and I decide to travel the country. And I go to northern Thailand. I go to Chiang Mai. I go to Chiang Rai. I go to a village in Khon Khan, and I have photos to put in of the village of Khon Khan, and that was the girl that I had first met when I moved there. We were off and on again for a couple of years. Eventually, she married a Norwegian man and moved to Norway.

And her name was Nuan, and I will never forget her. She was an integral part of my life, off and on, for a little while and inspired me to speak Thai. Because I would be on the telephone for ten minutes with a Thai dictionary trying to figure out one sentence to speak. And so in between my travels, I would go to Thai school and take private tutoring lessons for an hour or two a day, five to six days a week, and I would do that for three to four, maybe five months a year for about three years, and became proficient enough to speak Thai.

Eventually, I also went to school for reading and writing, which gave me a headache and I gave up on that. I no longer go to Thai school and I speak enough to get by when I need to, and if I travel in Thailand more in the future, maybe I will go back to school.

So eventually, I traveled all over Thailand. I will insert the story of Noi's Village up in Udon Thani. I traveled all over Udon

Thani, into the northern border of Burma and Laos. I can't remember the name of the town right on the border of Burma. There were very interesting temples. And I went to temples all over Thailand.

And one of the ways I traveled was, sometimes I flew, but a couple of times, I have taken taxis on 1,500, 2,000 mile trips, because I can take a taxi for $50 a day plus gas, and then I have a driver and a guide. So I drove taxis all over the country and stopped at every temple and interesting, small sites that I saw.

So I was a pretty adventurous person, and I did most of this, almost all of this traveling alone. I traveled to a place outside of Chiang Mai called oh, God. I am going to have to look at the story, but this is where we go to the crazy Thai wedding, and that was probably in 2005, 2006, I believe. I don't have all of the years straight and we will work it out later. That was absolute insanity. I took a taxi up into the mountains for this wedding. I was the best man there, and it was just a drunken, insane two day wedding.

Over the years, I have had a few different girlfriends over in Thailand. I have also visited many of the go go bars and massage parlors, and I continue to travel quite a bit over there, but not as much as I used to.

I first went there in the year 2000, 2001. It was very underdeveloped still. I went to the Killing Fields and the Phnom Penh prisons, and just a very incredible place to go. I went there for a travel visa when I was staying in Thailand for extra time, but

I am going to continue on Thailand. But Nuan was my first real girlfriend over there, and then I had a girlfriend, another girl whose name I can't remember. She ended up marrying somebody and moving to Finland. Oh, her name was Ta. And she spoke good English and had a degree in bookkeeping, but she

But in the beginning oh, I met a girl named Dang also. When I went there the very first time, I had gone online to try and meet a girl before I showed up, and I met a girl who ran a real estate office named Dang, and I still know her to this year, to this time, 12 years later.

She was a very nice girl and she spoke English and she was her job was to warn me not to fall into the trap of going with prostitutes or getting ripped off in Thailand. And eventually, I tried to find some businesses to go in with her. Fortunately, she was very, very honest, because she could have ripped me off for a lot of money and never did. She really steered me in the right direction. She was a really, really nice girl, and I wish all the best for her. She still lives in Phuket, Thailand.

I guess one of the things that interested me a lot was, I had never had any luck with romance in the United States, partly due to my drunkenness, but also my shyness, and in Thailand, I was able to get over that. Yes, a lot of the women over there are interested in white men who have a bank account, and I am one of those people, and I had been fairly financially successful with my business by the time I was traveling over there more also.

So I traveled all over the country. And as far as the girlfriends went, first, there was Nuan and then Ta, who I met in Pattaya, and we got along very well, but she ended up marrying somebody in Finland. A lot of the women that I met, after a period of time, if you don't want to get married, they move on, and I became very I got cold feet about getting married.

And then I had moved to Australia in 2003 and met Aidi, and we became very close for a long time. So I am back in Thailand now. I am traveling around Thailand in 2004. I am starting to buy condos. I am getting very involved in renovating condos and investing a lot of money in Thailand and learning the language.

I can't remember I don't think I had a solid girlfriend there for a couple of years. I was just involved in trying to get the business going over there and meeting new friends and got very involved in the 12 step work over there also.

Let's just face it. You know, it is going to be impossible not to break my anonymity. I got very involved in Alcoholics Anonymous over there and I got very involved with the Thai community and Alcoholics Anonymous in Thailand also. So that was a blessing, and I have been able to stay sober in that crazy country.

There are parts of Pattaya where I have lived, off and, on where one street after another is just lined with bars and girls screaming at you to come in and drink, so there is a lot of temptation there.

I first bought the condo in Jomtien, and less than a year later I met a woman named Sunisa. She was actually a cab driver for me, taking me to the airport, and she talked me into buying another condo in a building called the

Thip Building. I still own two condos there. Over the years, I probably renovated ten condominiums in that building.

Sunisa was a Thai who spoke perfect English, and she had worked her way up from working in a real estate office, to owning a couple of taxicabs, to renting out motorcycles, to having an Internet shop, to renting out condominiums for people and starting to do real estate deals.

And I got involved with her and we did a lot of deals together, and I gave her power of attorney, and she helped me a lot, and I made a lot of money in Thailand for a couple of years. Well, I don't know about a lot of money, but I made a little bit of money and did a lot of deals with Sunisa.

And, eventually, she got too big. She started to own dozens of condominiums. She almost bought most of Soi 7, where the Thip condo and the Thien Thong condo are. She owned, I believe, three restaurants and several of what we call shop houses. A shop house is a building that is usually three to four stories, has a business on the bottom and then two to three floors of rooms that you can either rent out or live in.

And she just she got overextended is what happened. And, eventually, what happened was she ripped off a lot of people and she almost ripped off me, and I ended up losing a lot of money. Probably lost as much as I made over the years. Who knows.

But some of the condos I bought from her, she bought back from me for less than I bought them from her. And just before she disappeared and she is now a fugitive from justice I became very irritated. I guess this was about 2008, 2009, and I basically went insane.

Yes. 2009, 2010, I was going back and forth to Thailand at that point. I was staying in Thailand seven, eight, nine months a year almost, and I was just going crazy with these renovations and with Sunisa and afraid I was going to lose everything.

And eventually after threatening her, threatening her family, threatening her grandchild, threatening to get a hold of her husband in Australia and revealing what she had done, going to her bank and making a scene, somehow, some way, I was able to get almost all of my money back from her. And within less than a month after that, with her owing well over a million dollars to several other people and ripping off several people's condominiums that had been entrusted to her through power of attorney, that she assigned over to other people or sold, she disappeared.

And it now has been three to four years and nobody has heard from her. So very strange. And I was friends with her and her family. I went to her wedding. I went to her daughter's wedding. I went to her son's wedding. And I thought that we were really, really good friends, but that has ended, and thank God I got most of that money back. I sold almost all of my condominiums.

At one point, I owned 11 condominiums in all at the same time, and I had all of my money invested in Thailand, and it became a source, a big source of irritation. Not too much time for love when that was going on.

So anyway, I got most of my money back to the United States, and as my friend Karl says, I try to take more of a middle path. I made some bad decisions, some bad business decisions during that time, but at least I didn't lose everything.

One of the things about Thailand I haven't mentioned is confrontation. People in Thailand do not accept confrontation. When I tell you I had this problem with Sunisa and I started screaming at her and threatening her and going into her bank and calling her names, people are looking at me like I am crazy.

You don't do things like that in Thailand. Everything is jai yin yin, which means keep a cool heart. When you go off the wall, people ignore you and they will no longer talk to you. So what happens is, at some point, you have to learn to go with the flow in Thailand.

One of the best ways to go with the flow is, don't get too involved. Don't get too involved in love. Don't get too involved in business. Just don't get too involved. But I have a pretty good life over there at the moment. I did fall in love with a girl named Noi. And Sunisa helped me with her too, because she didn't speak one word of English, and she lived in Udon Thani, but she had a brother that worked at a bar in Pattaya or in Jomtien, and I met her down there, and I just thought she was the best thing since sliced bread.

I had sworn I would never go to

another Thai village, because I was I am not meant for that little Thai village life. I will explain more about it, but when you go a to a Thai village, basically, you are in rice country, and there is no running water or toilets or real showers. You take a shower with a ladle of water and you take a crap or a piss in a hole in the ground and then dump water down that hole.

And I wasn't going to go back to a village. I had been to the village with Duan. I had been to the village for Jeff's wedding and also visited up there a couple of times, and I wasn't going back to a village. But four or five days after I met Noi, I found myself in a little village in the middle of nowhere in Udon Thani.

Chapter 20

Visiting Noi's Village

Written by Eddie

December 22nd, 2006

Yes, I am going to Noi's home. Why, why, why? Oh, yeah, I forgot how much I disliked all my previous visits to "the Village". Noi grows flowers and works part time as a cashier at a Karaoke bar about 5 miles outside the village... A real hoot.

My wonderful darling who turned out to be a nightmare.

Of course, I could have visited another nice college grad student's home or a bank teller lady's family with proper facilities, but no, I have to go to the outskirts of humanity. I am laughing at myself. It is definitely a place I could never live, but to be honest, most of the folks there seemed happy and were nice. I had made promises to myself before that I would NEVER visit the villages again.

After a couple of almost impossibly polite visits with upper class educated Thai girls, and meeting the parents, discussing future plans and being so proper, I was stiff with posture and scared to death of saying the wrong thing. Yes, most of the very nice educated ladies I have met DO bring one or both parents with them to meet the first time.

Noi says everything very cheap in her village. No spend much money. Of course she does not speak one word of English, and I'm busting my brain to speak my very best Thai, which is about equal to that of a three year old child.

I was thinking it would be a good idea to rent a car at the airport in Udon or hire driver… Oh, no, say Noi. I have friend pick up up. Driver too much money. Well, what a great idea. So the friend shows up with 6 other friends and we cram into his truck and shortly thereafter stop at a very nice little pond to eat. Of course the Farang pays for everything and it's about 1,800 baht for all the fish, shrimp, booze, etc. Haha.

Guess I decided it was time to go to the opposite spectrum, but I still had to meet Noi's mom.

Well, guys, I am truly in another world right now. I should have known when I started down the road to her home that I had made a big mistake, one that I have made before, but seem to forget every couple of years that I really should not be going to a girl's home to visit the family.

I have gone to Noi's home, and it is much much much different than even I imagined. I have been to small villages before, but I think this one tops it all. It's a rolling hills area with very, very small thatched roof homes. The home that Noi was born in and has lived in for 30 years is no bigger than many bathrooms. I would say maybe 150 square feet inside, built on stilts and just a few pieces of cheap would on the outside with palm leaves on the top. A make shift homemade ladder is used to climb into the home, two beds inside with mosquito nets, and a bed on the porch. Underneath the house there are hanging hammocks. A family of 6 or 7 live here. the bathroom is a small block structure in back with a squat toilet and couple buckets of water.

They grow about 2 or 3 acres of flowers to sell, and appear to make a decent living from that. They are all happy, mostly shoeless and carless. Have a couple bikes. There is a small outdoor kitchen. and yes, I have photo documentation of all this. Of course all the relatives show up to meet me. You could tell they had had their hair done and really tried to look their best even though they live in the most primitive conditions that I could ever imagine.

Yes, there is a full kitchen available also.

Everyone was quite kind and friendly. They gave me a chair while everyone else sat on mats on the ground and shared food and drink. Oh, yeah, of course, the Farang buys all the whiskey, beer and food for every lost family member. and it can get quite expensive. This is a good point to make.

While village life is cheap, when a farang comes to town, the expectation can be on him to treat all and sundry to a nice meal, unlimited alcohol as well as stock up the pantry with food for the next week as well as finance any new appliances

Depending on the time of the day the mats would be moved to more shade or a cooler area. There were a few toddlers half naked just running wild with a couple wild puppies. Haha. The whole village and this area are spectacularly beautiful and peaceful with most of the folks in the are growing flowers, rice and running other small businesses. We are on our way out to karaoke now. Already check in to a gorgeous Thai cottage on a lake that equals the nicest environment of any hotel I have ever stayed at for 450 baht per night. Anyway, the whole thing is turning into quite a lovely experience.

Well, at least I thought it MIGHT be. haha

Now to the karaoke… this should really be fun. Wow where did all these people come from.

They must be spending a lot of money. There is whiskey and beer bottles everywhere. Everybody is so nice. It's very hard to hear with all the music and singing. Noi has a lovely voice. Wow, tons of food coming to our table too. I wonder who is ordering all this food? Such nice people.

Well, it's getting late and time to go back to our lovely cottage. Check, please?

2000 baht! What? Yes, the farang is buying everything for everybody. haha.

Very difficult for me to keep my cool, but I did. Okay, first night. I won't allow this to happen again. Yeah, sure.

So the next day we go to Nongkhai near the Laos Border and I quite enjoyed the day.

There's a long story behind this place, and I have all the info on it, but I won't bore you with the details.

To be fair, Noi and her friends did take me to many nice places and I have hundreds of photos of the countryside and national parks, streams and waterfalls. It was very enjoyable, but somehow for three days, it seemed every time we sat down to eat there would end up being a huge bill where I was not only paying for the food and liquor that were all consuming at that moment, but later I learned they were ordering bags of food to take with them also. Yes, I did like Noi very much, and for a rare few days allowed myself to be taken advantage of.

It was a very good learning experience, and I did see many sights and meet many people that I never would have met on a tour. Frankly, I knew that I would be spending a lot of money there, and it probably would NOT have bothered me if there had not been so much drinking leading to squabbles and fights, and even one night a family member knocking on our cottage door and 2:30 in the morning asking for money.

Noi truly was a very very nice person, but I just can't handle her family, her life and everything that would go along with her .Of course she wants to spend the rest of her life with me. I have been single my whole life and will stay that way.

I will still talk to Noi now and then. She is crushed that I do not want to go back to her home, or for that matter, do NOT even want her to visit me in Jomtien. But it was another one of those experiences that is best to only experience one time. Haha. So those who read this know, I am not a newbie. I spend much of my life in Thailand, speak the language, have a condo here and have dated women from every walk of life. Just one of those things I got caught up in, and wrote about it to laugh at myself and maybe give a bit of a warning to anyone thinking of visiting their new honey's village.

Peace and love,

Khun Eddie (Village Peaceman)

Stickman's thoughts:

> Really nice submission and I liked the photos a lot.

I just thought she was fantastic, but she turned out to be a drunken alcoholic, in my opinion, and things did not work out. Things did not work out. And after I read the insert that we are going to put in here, I will decide if anything else needs to be added to that. But that was a very aggravating time in my life, where I thought

I had fallen in love, when in less than two weeks I realized that it was wrong and extricated myself from it.

Currently, I met a girl three and a half years ago, so that would have been about 2009. Her name, I thought, was Nes, but she has several different names. And as far as names go in Thailand, most girls have long names. I am not even going to try to pronounce them, but they are usually very long names that you can't spell or pronounce, and everybody is given a nickname.

And so you will meet Noi, Nok, Lek, Nes, Ta, Nim, Pim, Porn, Pawn. Everybody seems to have a two to a three letter name. And so if you are keeping a phone book or you are meeting a lot of people, you will soon know three or four Leks and five Nois, and it is kind of funny.

So anyway, I met a girl named Nes. Her real name was Pattama Ngamnongor. So now you have a long name. And I can spell that for you. P a t t a m a N g a m n o n g o r. And she lives in a village, Roi Et, and I have not been to that village yet. I have known her for three and a half years and I haven't been to that village yet, and eventually I will probably go there.

I have another friend named Skip, who I put him online on a Thai Lovelinks line, and he met a girl who lives in Udon Thani. She is a professor at a government university, and he has now lived up in Udon Thani for three or four years. So that is another whole story that I should probably write about.

Anyway, I have been with now I call her Da or Nes for three and a half years. For about the first two years, we broke up and got together a couple of times, and now we have been solidly together for about a year and a half. And she has been real sweet and I really like her a lot.

She is a lot younger than me, but that doesn't bother me and it doesn't seem to bother people in Thailand, but I am sure that if I brought her to the United States, I would be getting a lot of stares.

The men would be staring either because they were envious or thought I was crazy, and the women would be staring because they would think I was a pervert. And also, I think a lot of European or American women are very upset with the fact that a man can go to

Thailand and meet a woman half his age and seem to settle down and have a good life with a good looking, younger woman who will take better care of him than a lot of American women would.

And part of it doesn't seem right. Of course, it doesn't seem right to an older white woman, but it seems really right to an older white guy who is trying to relive his past, and I have been able to relive my past in Thailand.

You know, I grew up wanting to be a rock 'n' roll star and have the whole thing, the drugs, sex, rock 'n' roll, and lots of women, and relive those stories you hear of Led Zeppelin and the Rolling Stones and Ozzie Osborne and Jim Morrison.

And I gave up the drugs and the sex, and I don't have too much rock 'n' roll anymore. I do play a little guitar, but I gave up the drugs and the booze. I shouldn't say I gave up the sex, but I did give up the drugs and the booze and a lot of the rock 'n' roll, but I have I have a penchant for lust and romance all wrapped up into one, and I found that in Thailand, and that is something that you have to be very careful with.

It has brought a lot of men to their

destruction, so I try to keep a balance of living in the United States and running a successful business over here and keeping my girlfriend in Thailand and enjoying what Thailand has to offer, and I think over the years I've found a pretty good balance.

I am not as involved in going to go go bars every night and going out to see all of the pleasures of flesh and all of the things that a lot of guys go to Thailand for now, although I enjoy a beautiful woman, as most men do.

So this is going to be edited a lot, because I have no idea what this is going to look like on paper. I have a love hate relationship with Thailand. I just don't know what else to say about it right now.

But I have a feeling I will be going back and forth for years to come, number one, because I do love Thai women, and also, I have a lot of money, I have money invested over there in condominiums, which I could stand to either lose some money or make a tiny bit of money.

Chapter 21

Cambodia

In 2001, I went to Cambodia after I read a book called Guns, Girls and Ganja. Cambodia was mostly undeveloped at that time. All of the streets in Phnom Penh and most of the places I went to were still dirt. They had water trucks that would come around and spray the streets a couple of times a week to try to keep the dust down.

I did all of the tourist things. I went to what they called The Gun Range. You could throw a hand grenade. You could shoot machine guns. You could do anything you wanted. And I have photos of myself standing on this gun range with this array of weapons.

I went to the Killing Fields, and I have photos of myself standing with a hundred skulls. I saw the tree that they would smash babies against. I went to the prisons and saw the electrical wires out of the they called it the reeducation camps, and the little, tiny cots that people slept on in little, tiny rooms with electrical shock treatment that they had to go through, with their photos up all around the room, and I took photos of all of that also.

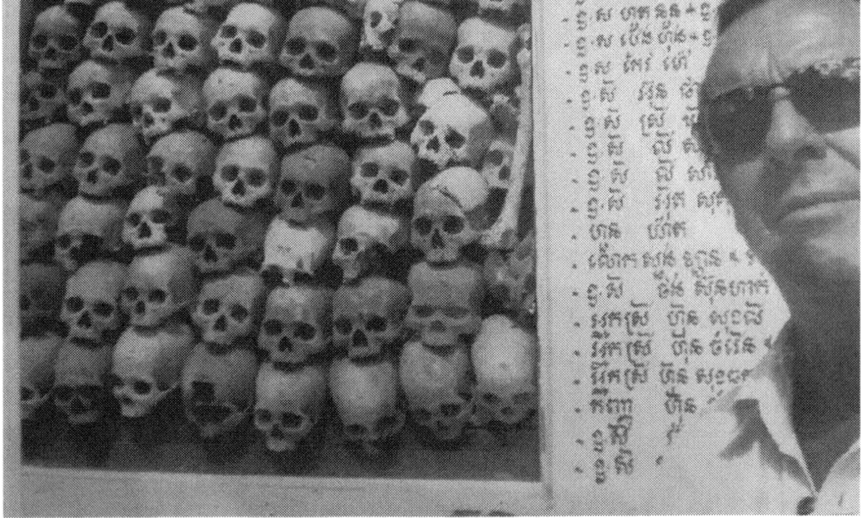

Cambodia, Khmer Rouge Killing Fields

I have been to Cambodia maybe, I don't know, maybe seven or eight times. And Phnom Penh, in my opinion, was a shit hole. It has been upgraded quite a bit. Most of the roads have all been improved. They have a nice road that goes from Phnom Penh all the way to Sihanoukville, which is a seaside community that is also a shit hole, but has casinos and they are building up hotels and making a little beach resort there, and that will eventually probably be very nice too.

They just put in traffic lights a few years ago, which nobody pays attention to. They just run right through them. But I had fun in Phnom Penh and in Sihanoukville. As I would say, "Edward went to a house of ill repute there." A lot of strange things.

You will hear all kinds of stories about Phnom Penh, about pedophiles, going there and everything, and I don't know anything about that. But what I found most interesting was, it is such a poor country, and if you give a penny to a beggar, you have got 30 people tugging at your pants, you know, asking for more money. You have to be really careful.

I hired a guide and went to a place called Angkor Wat. It's one of the seven wonders of the world. It is one of the largest Buddhist temples in the world, and it was uncovered some time in the last century. It had been overgrown by jungles.

It would take two or three days just to walk around the entire grounds and have it all explained to you, and the entire temple is engraved with drawings that can all be explained. It is like hieroglyphics that talk about the history of Cambodia, and it is extremely interesting. I will definitely go back there and then take more time. I only did a one day tour and I would like to do a three day tour, maybe even longer, of Siem Reap and the Angkor Wat area.

I also went to an artist community up there that was developed for people with not only physical disabilities but mental disabilities.

Another thing you will notice right away. I have been to the border maybe 20 times, the border of Cambodia for visa runs, to get visas for Thailand, and there are hundreds of people missing arms and legs, mostly from the Khmer Rouge and from when Pol Pot was in power. There were a lot of, I guess, explosives around and so forth. And it is just really unusual to see everywhere. I have seen people with no arms and no legs, you know, going around on a roller board, either being pushed or rolling themselves on stumps.

I have seen children, five, six, seven year old children carrying three to six month old babies around. You don't know who is taking care of who. When you stay in Phnom Penh, there is the Mekong River that goes through there, and hundreds of people, just homeless people live on that river. Some have a little boat to live on. Some just live on the shoreline. And they brush their teeth, bathe and wash their clothes all in the same muddy, crappy river right there.

There is a nice boardwalk there and you can walk up and down that boardwalk, and kids will bother the heck out of you for money. You can't give them anything or you will just get pestered for the rest of your stay in Phnom Penh. It is probably one of the most least attractive things of Phnom Penh is the beggars.

What I did do a few times while I was over there, as the kids start to encroach on you and they all want money, is I will take them to a food stand or a restaurant and tell the restaurant to give everybody something to eat and feed all of them.

And I have photos of all of this. And the markets in Phnom Penh, just absolutely incredible. The smells will almost knock you out. And they sell anything that lives, dies, crawls, breathes or grows in these markets. Snakes, lizards, frogs, turtles, eggs, bugs, I mean, all kinds of strange meat and all kinds of strange smells. It is really, really a different world.

And the book Guns, Girls and Ganja, I recommend for people to read. That book was probably written in the late nineties, just before I went there, and that era of what it was like because it was just a lawless society was just ending about the time I went there.

They still had signs at the doors on some of the bars that said: Leave your weapons in the locker. They provided lockers for people to leave their guns and knives in before you go into the bar. So it was a very interesting experience traveling to Cambodia for me for the first time.

The last time I went there, I drove there, actually, with a friend and stayed in the seaside community of Sihanoukville for a week, and it was very nice. We went to some lovely beaches. I rented a motorcycle to drive around and went to the casinos, stayed in a nice hotel and had a lot of good food and really enjoyed myself there.

Chapter 22

Edward goes to the Philippines

Okay. So about 2007, maybe, I decided to go to the Philippines. I took a flight there from Thailand, got to Angeles City. Within hours, I wanted to turn around and leave. I thought it was the worst crap hole I had ever been in in my life.

After a couple of days of hanging out there and meeting some women, I changed my mind. I really did enjoy the women in the Philippines. So talking in the third sense, Edward really enjoyed the nightlife of the Philippines. And they had some nice shopping malls, and I don't really know what else to say about it, but since then, I have made about five trips back, and I have been to a place called Cebu City, which is interesting.

I went to Cloud 9 Resort. I was going to learn how to surf there. I met my friend Richard and the Filipina that he was going to marry, or that he did marry. At that time, they were engaged. I met them on the island of Cloud 9 Resort, and that was quite an interesting trip.

From that island, we took a little boat to another little deserted island. And it was just a real, real nice trip. Again, I went back with Richard and his wife last year, and we went to a place called La Union Surf Resort. Unfortunately, I hurt my back and I couldn't surf. I did try one day, but I was unsuccessful. And I enjoy the Philippines a lot. It is a beautiful place.

Chapter 23

Love, Romance, Lust, Love, Romance and Depression. Love, Lust, Romance, Heartbreak.

So my first girlfriend, really, that I can kind of remember was Barbara Wetzel. She had a twin sister named Pam Wetzel, so I was always kind of confused. But I met her in fifth or sixth grade, and we used to just walk home from school together, and I was kind of obsessed with her.

And then there were a couple of girls I liked in junior high, but nothing really ever happened. Junior high for us was seventh, eighth and ninth grade. I started drinking when I was in the eighth or ninth grade, and that switched things around a little bit.

I started high school in the tenth grade. And after I got a motorcycle eventually, I would take a girl up to the hills and get drunk and make out and touch each other and play around.

What happened when I was about 18 was, I did go to a couple of parties. I mean, I didn't fall in love with anybody. Let's just put it that way. I didn't fall in love with anybody. When I was about 18, I was taking a night school class in pottery, and I met a lady from South America, and one night, she brought her daughter there. Her daughter was about 15 or 16 years old.

Her name was Ljubica Bregamo, and I fell in love with that girl, and we started dating and it was wonderful. And I really thought that we would get married. We gave each other promise rings. We went out for a long time. She was a virgin, and I feel like I lost my virginity with her, for sure. She was the first girl that I ever had sex with that I was in love with, and she lost her virginity with me, and we had sex twice a day, and loved it.

It was just a wonderful, wonderful, wonderful experience, and I remember it to this day. I really thought I would spend the rest of my life with that girl. Unfortunately, what happened is, I was playing with the band and I started meeting other girls. And I went from I lost the gratitude that I had for being with one girl that I was in love with and I started cheating on her, and eventually she started cheating on me. I didn't even know about it, and I probably didn't care, because I was going out with so many other women.

And what happened was eventually she left me for another man a couple of years later, and she moved to Lake Tahoe. And my heart was broken so badly. I can't even tell you how. It just it is hard to explain, you know, when you love somebody as much as I thought I loved somebody and been so stupid to have lost them.

Eventually, a year or so after that, I moved to Lake Tahoe after I a had a lung and a heart problem. I moved to Tahoe for a job captioning, thinking that somehow I mean, I was stalking her, but I wasn't looking for her. And eventually one day, somehow, we got in contact with each other, and we did meet at a casino in South Lake Tahoe. I don't remember if she brought her boyfriend with her or not, but we met for a short while.

And even four or five years later after that, we got together one night and had sex. And as I recall, it wasn't that good. At that point, she was engaged to, I believe, a doctor, a Spanish doctor in Panorama City, and I believe she married him and they are still together.

I saw her once maybe since then, maybe when I was about 32. We saw each other one night, and I hope she still thinks about me. After Ljubica, I didn't have any love for a long time. I went out with a girl named Maryann Ortega. Apparently, she thought we were getting married. I never had any such intentions.

I then fell in love with a Filipino Swedish girl. She looked pure Filipino. Her mother was Swedish. Her father was Filipino. And I would have been about 24 at that time. And we were hot, hot, hot and heavy. And what happened was, she had an affair with my mailman, broke my heart.

That broken heart didn't last as long as the Ljubica broken heart. I don't think to this day I have ever gotten over that one. After her, at one point, I met a young girl who was a hostess at IHOP. Her name was Linda Guidry, and I started dating her. And she was as close to a virgin as you can get. She was young too, maybe 17, 18 at the most, and I was 24.

And we went out, off and on, for a long time. I was never faithful. She moved in with me at one point when I was about 26 or 27, and we broke up again, and then she started dating somebody else and I got jealous and I begged her to marry me, and that was a mistake.

I think after we changed the wedding invitations three times, I finally married her, and I told this story already. I got drunk in a bar and finally made it to the wedding altar that morning and got married and threw up at the reception and took her out drinking all night and then to Mexico and asked for an annulment.

We were together a little bit. We moved into a motor home together shortly after that, and then we broke up and got back together and moved into an apartment for a little while, but it was a very volatile relationship, and we broke up. We got an annulment.

I was in a real depression then for a long time. And then I met a girl named Susan Anders. And I kind of was in love with her, but I was also obsessed with a cocktail waitress at my bowling alley. So that didn't really work out. I was having an affair with a cocktail waitress while I was dating Susan Anders, and she found out and she ended up marrying our drummer, a man named Tom.

So, really, a lot of strange and then I didn't date for about a year, until I moved to Boston, and then I fell in love with my supervisor, Suzanne Estofi, and I still have very, very fond feelings of her. I didn't contact her for almost 20 years, probably over 20 years after I left Boston, and she is up in Maine now.

What happened was, she was married when I met her. She divorced her husband for me. When she realized that my drinking was more important than anything else in my life and that I was also a serial adulterer I basically stayed out all night at least three or four nights a week playing with different bands and meeting other women, and then staying with her the other two or three nights a week.

It just wasn't going to work out, obviously, and she decided not move to California with me unless I could prove that I could go 30 days without drinking. And I thought I made it one day. I didn't really think I made it one day. I told her I made it one day, but she saw my car in the parking lot of a bar and called me on it.

So we broke up. While I was in Boston, there were also a couple of other women that I went out with, but it was insignificant because it didn't last. When I came to San Diego, believe it or not, I fell in love within the first week I was here, and she was really lovely. She was a waitress at a place called Potato Shack in Encinitas.

I met her on the beach, and I really thought we had something going, and within a couple of weeks, we were laying in bed one night and she got a call from Hawaii, and it was her ex boyfriend, who had broken her heart, and decided he wanted to get back together with her.

So that was crushing. And shortly after that, I met a girl named Kathryn or Cathy, I believe. And she was perfect, because I met her in a bar and she drank like me. She was a fiery Irish girl, and she was great in the sack and we got along really good.

One night, she was following me home from the bar and I looked up and I saw red lights and she had gotten pulled over and gotten a driving under the influence. I was too drunk to stop too, so a few hours later, I went down to the police station to get her out of jail, and I was lucky I got out of there in one piece too. She was still screaming at the cops. Anyway, eventually, she cheated on me and moved and that was over.

Our tape is almost over. I will see what else I can stick in here. After that, I met another girl in a bar named Debra Frase, and she ended up moving in with me. We had about a two year affair, and the cocaine started getting in the way of us also.

And I almost married her. Thank God I didn't. But that was kind of the end of having anything that looked like a real girlfriend, and I have only had one real girlfriend in the United States maybe since then, and that was well, I had a girl named Jeanine that lived with me, off and on, but we were just out of our minds drunk and stoned constantly. It wasn't really a relationship. It was just two people that got fucked up together.

And then when I was about a year and a half sober, I met Jennifer, and we got engaged, and I got broken hearted over that too. So I pretty much gave up on searching for love until I went to Thailand, and that story comes up in Thailand. But here I am. I am 58 years old, I am still single, no kids and no plans to ever get married.

I will now get into the story of drunkenness and sobriety, since it is one of the most important things of my life. I probably mentioned one of the first times I ever got drunk, I was about 13 and I chugged a bunch of hard liquor with a friend, had a drinking contest over at Gina and Terry's house, and I got semi naked with Gina and was able to touch her and do some things I had never done in my life, and it was the best day of my life.

And I ended up getting into a blackout and probably almost dying riding my bicycle up a four lane busy street and passing out next to a corn field and going to the hospital with alcohol poisoning.

And over the years, from that time on, I got in trouble drinking a lot. I didn't always get in trouble, but every time I got in trouble, I had been drinking. And I had a love affair with booze, and it was just something I really liked a lot and it helped me.

Booze helped me be able to talk to girls. It helped me be able to dance, but unfortunately, a lot of times at bars, by the time I had drank enough booze to ask a girl to dance, to get up the nerve to ask somebody, I had had too much to drink already.

I suffered from extreme shyness. I was a singer and a guitar player in a band, and I was just so shy, I couldn't even get on stage and sing, and liquor helped get me ready to do that.

So I always loved drinking, and eventually, I started smoking a lot of marijuana also. So marijuana and booze was just a normal part of my life. I can't remember I mean, from age 13 to 16 or 17, maybe it was mostly only on the weekends, in the summertime and holidays, but by 18 or 19, it was every day. I mean, I just never went past lunchtime without a drink.

At one point in my life, I said: Okay. We have a two drink limit at lunch. Because I found whenever I had more than two or three drinks, when I got to three or four, I would be a little too messed up when I got back from work.

At one point in my mid twenties, when I was doing research and development for DigiText in Santa Monica, I used to go out and just get hammered. And the company didn't really care that I did, because I would come back and still be able to work most of the time, at least in the office. I couldn't have if I was in a court reporter situation, but I was working in an office.

But what they didn't like was if I took other people from the office out with me, that they would get so plastered they either had to go home or get sick, so they asked me not to take other people out drinking with me.

So, well, a typical day would have been I didn't smoke dope in the morning because it made me too tired, but a typical day would be, I would either have a beer or a vodka and orange juice in the morning before I left home, and then I would drive 30 miles to work from the hills.

I either lived in Topanga Canyon or Box Canyon and I would drive 30 miles to work, and I would work for a while, and then at lunchtime go out and have two drinks, sometimes three, and then go back to work and, at some point, take a break in the afternoon, maybe smoke a little bit of dope.

I kept an ice chest in the back of my car, and on the way home, I would mix up some cocktails that I would, instead of taking the freeway, I would take the Coast Highway, Highway 1, up the coast to Topanga Canyon, and I would drink up the coast.

And if my cup got empty, I would stop at a gas station and get a couple of dollars worth of gas and mix myself a new cocktail, light up a joint and go, because a lot of times, it was at least an hour drive.

So I got my drink, my joint, a few cigarettes and then home. And then I am up in the hills, and when I get home, I drink, or I stop and go to a happy hour and meet my friends for happy hour. And then several nights a week, before the band kicked me out, I would be over at the studio playing and singing with the band.

So that was my drinking. And what happened was, you know, I wouldn't say I was under control, but I didn't really care about my drinking that much until I had the problem with my heart and my lung, and I said I am going to quit drinking and smoking.

And when I found out I just couldn't quit, I guess because I was addicted, I kind of lost hope. I gave up hope, you know. And a doctor at one point had told me, you know, that I probably wouldn't have a long life if I continued this lifestyle.

And Jim Morrison was a big idol of mine. By the way, I am going to go see him in Paris, France in September. At least I am going to see his grave. I just thought, well, I will die like Jim Morrison. I will drink and I will die when I am 27 and that will be over.

So I got into really, really heavy drinking in my mid twenties. After 28 and I had Linda and I started to get married, I said I want to get my career together and have kids. And I started working really hard, and I would say that I drank only beer probably at least four nights a week and didn't drink tequila or whiskey, except three nights a week.

I tried not to get drunk every day.

I drank every day, but I tried not to get drunk every day. And I would say I was even being semi functional, I seemed to perform very well. I was just really good at work. I was really good at stenography, and I had a heavy work ethic.

I mean, if they needed me ten or twelve hours a day to do input, to get captioning done, I stayed and I got it done, drunk or not.

So that was kind of how my drinking thing went. And when I went to Boston, I was already out of control before I got there, but I became more out of control, because I became indispensable, and when you are an indispensable alcoholic, that is trouble. Because what they said to me straight up was you know, they would catch me drinking in the office and I passed out on every job I have ever been at. At one point or another, the boss has found me passed out on the floor in an office.

But they said, Hey, whatever it takes to keep you here. So I was allowed to drink in the office there, and I would take long breaks and go to the bar down the street and get drunk and come back to the office and closed caption my show.

And I can't really oh, the only way I can explain closed captioning in a book is to tell you, I sit and I either watch TV or I listen to a TV news broadcast, either news or a sporting event, some type of live event, and I type real time using a court reporting machine, a stenograph machine everything that they are saying, and it has to be done with 99.5 percent accuracy, at least, I would say.

So as my girlfriend in Boston said, who was also my supervisor, she found it quite amazing that I could drink so much and still perform my job. But eventually, it did catch up with me, and it became harder and harder to closed caption and drink the amount of liquor I was drinking.

And then when I moved to San Diego, I was only working about an hour a day for the first year or so, and so the drinking didn't get in the way. Actually, the job started to get in the way of my drinking. It was like, oh, gosh, I have to go to work for an hour now.

So I had to try to be careful not to get too drunk before 5:00 o'clock in the afternoon, but I wasn't always successful at that. Many, many, many days, I would say hundreds of days when I worked at Media Captioning, when I was a full time employee there and getting paid to be a full time employee, I would go in at 2:00

o'clock in the afternoon with a hideous hangover, having already drank a couple of beers, work for about an hour, go into a side office, fall asleep for an hour or two and take a nap, which they allowed me to do, wake up, then closed caption CNN, Larry King Live or whatever else I was working on, do a good job, and finish up and leave by 7:00 or 8:00 o'clock at night.

I mean, I wasn't putting in more than a few hours a day for full time pay. And eventually, as the company grew and I was not as I became less indispensable everywhere I went, and when you become less indispensable, you are easy to let go. So I was fired three times from that company, but I was hired back three times, so there was something about me that they liked.

And then when I added cocaine to the mix, it even got worse, because now I am not getting enough sleep. I am staying up all night, or at least half the night. I am rarely sleeping more than two or three hours at night and then getting up and trying to work. And eventually, I just couldn't work anymore.

So that was how my and I had started going to AA. I was sent to meetings once when I was 16 when I got in trouble. They were like I won't even describe the meetings, but they were like Alcoholic meetings. I think it was like a diversion program.

And then I had to go to some meetings again in my twenties a couple of times, and then I went to AA meetings when I was in my late twenties with Danny Wright, who died with a gutful of vodka in him, just drank himself to death.

And, you know, I just thought they were stupid. I mean, let's part of this chapter will be called this chapter could be called Alcoholic, AA Crap no. AA Hocus pocus.

So I thought AA was just for real wimps. And, in fact, our band, when we were playing, used to call ourselves Known Alcoholics, and when we wanted a drink we would go: Ka, Ka, Ka. KA rules! And anybody in Alcoholics Anonymous is a wimp.

We would humiliate people that we knew that gave up drinking and gone to Alcoholics Anonymous. Once again, I drove to a few meetings of Alcoholics Anonymous in Boston to take a friend there who was court ordered, and he killed himself.

So in my mind, I am like, look what

happens. You go to Alcoholics Anonymous. They make you feel guilty for drinking and then you die.

At the age of 35 in San Diego, I voluntarily started going to Alcoholics Anonymous again, and it was just out of sheer desperation. And what I found was, there was a part of it I liked.

The part of it I liked was, there were some people there that I knew who had drank like I had and who were sober, but what I didn't like was that they don't drink at all. They have these stupid rules, not even beer, not even weed. And they would say stuff to me like you smell like you have been drinking.

And I am like, All I had was a couple of beers. Well, we don't drink at all. I was like, you are kidding me?

And then they are talking about praying and getting on their knees and doing these stupid steps, and Bill Wilson, and it just it was very cultish to me. It still is, to this day, but I love it now.

So I am going to these AA groups and also to some cocaine groups, Cocaine Anonymous, and I just I am besides myself, because I like some of the people there, but I don't like this whole thing, like you have got to raise your hand if you are new, and then somebody says they have a year or five years. You are full of shit. You haven't got five years. And I started seeing people in the bars. Well, maybe one out of 200. Every now and then, I would see somebody in a bar that I had seen in a meeting who had taken a token for time. They have tokens for one year, two years, three years, 30 days, 60 days, 90 days.

I'd go, Man, didn't you just take a token for two years of being sober, and now you are in here drinking?

Oh, don't tell anybody you saw me.

What a bunch of crap. And so what happens is, when you go to Alcoholics Anonymous or one of these 12 step programs, you earn time. And it is strange, because it makes it a hierarchy, and they say we are all the same, it is all one day at a time, but yet there is a guy with 30 days or who is new, and there is a guy with five years, so we would look up to the guy with five years, and it is kind of that way.

I am now clean and sober 15 years without putting anything in my body, no pot, no pills, no booze, no nothing, and so I guess I am an old timer now. But at the time, I just thought it was so stupid.

And I went to these meetings off and on. I would say finally about 1992, I got almost two months of sobriety. And I started really liking it, but I said, you know what? Screw it. And I went out drinking again.

And I came back to the meetings once in a while. Sometimes I got serious. I came back and forth to the meetings until I didn't ever get time again. 1996, when I came back from Pittsburgh, I got 90 days, 119 days. And then April 10th, 1997 was the day that I went to a detox center and moved into sober living and I have been sober ever since.

So that was what it was like drinking. And I will say the last ten years, a lot of the time, I just wanted to die. I mean, I just wished the days would end. I wanted it to all be over, and one of the reasons I tried so hard to get sober finally in the end was because I was scared it wasn't going to end.

I couldn't take my life. I didn't have the balls to shoot myself or gas myself, and I just hated my life and I hated myself and everybody hated me. I had no friends, no money, no food, no family. I wasn't sure where I was going to live. It was just an absolute living nightmare.

So I raised up the white flag and I gave my life to Alcoholics Anonymous, and it has been a really wonderful ride. It seemed hopeless kind of at first. I mean, I am living in a little room with nothing but a sleeping bag and a lamp and a big book, and I started doing what they asked me to do in Alcoholics Anonymous.

I started praying and I started doing the steps and I got a sponsor and I started sponsoring people. I started making coffee and helping out and getting involved in events. And what happened was, I became an honest, good person, basically, and I made amends for all of the wrongs I had done in the past. Many people couldn't believe it. I paid back all the money that I owed. I tried to make things right with people that I had hurt physically and emotionally.

It took 12 years with my sister, but she now loves me and we have a good relationship. She just couldn't believe that I would ever change because I had hurt her and the family for so long, and so it has been nice to get good with the family again.

My mother was so scared of me, she left San Diego and moved to Oregon with my sister, and she was scared to ever see what would happen if I had another relapse, but we have a very loving relationship.

Mom in her model pose

I got to be you know, my father was somebody who I thought was so disappointed in me, and I hated him for that, and we never had a close relationship, and after I got sober, we got to be friends for the last two years of his life, and so that was really good too.

My Father overseas on business, Cairo 1946

What's happened mostly in Alcoholics Anonymous that has been so good is I have been able to, obviously, lead a sober life, but I have been able to lead an honest life. I don't have to hide anymore. I am able to have real friends, good friends.

I never did get the love of my life and the marriage and the kids, but it doesn't matter because I love my life and I am happy with the person that I am. I am really happy I have my mother and my sister back in my life. And I have traveled all over the world since I got sober. You have read about it or heard about it from this what I have written so far in this book.

I have made 50 international flights around the world. I have become respected in the closed captioning industry again. I have saved a lot of money and been able to put together a little a little bit of security for the future. I am not wealthy, but I am surprised to have anything at all. And I have just so much gratitude in my life, for the life that I have been given in sobriety.

We are not supposed to talk about the good deeds that we will do, but I will say that I have tried, to the best of my ability, and succeeded in many ways in being a good person and helping a lot of other alcoholics and drug addicts get clean and sober.

And I have tried to carry the message, the experience that I have had in my life to other people that are in treatment centers and detox centers and people that walk into Alcoholics Anonymous who feel the same hopelessness that I felt.

And I have been able to watch a lot of people get sober and change their lives, and that is what happens in Alcoholics Anonymous if you really give yourself to the program is you get a new life.

And you don't have to buy the whole program lock, stock and barrel. I didn't, but I did do everything they asked me to do when I finally got back. And after you get some time under your belt, you can speak your own mind in a meeting of Alcoholics Anonymous.

But I have good friends in AA today and, you know, I don't hang out in the bars. I mean, I can go to a bar. It is no problem. If I do go to a bar, I usually go with somebody who is in AA, but every day, I talk to other sober people. And one of the I don't know. It is just a good thing in my life.

And most of the people I used to talk to before I got sober, I was talking to them with a bottle in front of me or a guitar in my hand, and we talked about music and booze and women, but we never talked about our feelings. And we talk about our feelings and our lives and things that we are grateful for and the things that we are sad about, and it has just opened up a whole new way of life to me, which I am really, really grateful for and really happy about.

So that is my pitch on what it was like to be drunk and what it is like to be sober, and I don't know what the next chapter is going to be. I have already written about love and romance and heartbreak.

Okay. So I am just talking to myself now trying to figure out how to end this up. I guess what it all boils down to, it appeared that I might have had an idyllic childhood that I turned into a pile of shit, because I always thought people expected too much of me.

One part of me was very smart and very athletic and another part was shy and embarrassed. The booze kind of took me down the wrong road and hanging out with the wrong people. My dream of being a great musician never materialized because I didn't put out the work for it to happen.

As a direct result, even though I finished college and was a talented court reporter, I became a half ass musician and a half ass court reporter and had no self esteem. As a direct result of having no self esteem, I couldn't put together a decent relationship with another woman.

And fortunately, I had enough talent that I was able to keep moving and finding new places to live and make new friends and get new jobs, and I always had a strong work ethic too.

I am real happy with the way everything ended up, eventually getting sober at the age of 42 and now going on 58. I am very happy with the life I have today. I live in a one bedroom apartment in Encinitas, California, North County, San Diego near the beach. I walk on the beach every day.

I have some good friends. I travel to Thailand two or three times a year. I've traveled to many other places also. In the last four or five years, I have been to Indonesia, South America, Australia, Philippines, Cambodia, Thailand.

I am going to Paris shortly in September to say hi to Jim Morrison's grave and give him his soul back that I thought was transferred into my body during a stage of drunken psychosis.

I also plan to keep trying to learn how to surf. I haven't really learned to surf, but I will insert some photos from my trip to the Gold Coast in 2010, where my reunion with my last girlfriend in Australia Aidi didn't go well.

Anyway, maybe I will call her tonight and see what is going on with her. I am on Facebook and I put my life on Facebook. I just really don't know what else to say right now at this time.

I am just real grateful that life has turned out the way that it has and that I have come to respect myself and enjoy who I am and what I am doing with my life today. And then with that, I will say peace, love and harmony to all.

Photographs

Surfing with Milton

My Grandfather

Me and my Grandfather and Sister

age 19

Eddie at 8 or 9 years old

Made in the USA
Las Vegas, NV
07 March 2024